Y0-BQS-412

The Man I Knew
Was
Once A Boy

The Letters of Herbert Barness,
1938-1948

Edited by Lynda Barness

Copyright

© 2015 by Lynda Barness

All Rights Reserved. No part of this publication may be used or repro-
duced in any form or by any means, graphic, electronic, or mechanical, including scanning, photocopying, recording, taping, or by any information
storage retrieval system or otherwise, without prior written permission of
the copyright holder except in the case of brief quotations as part of critical
articles or reviews.

ISBN-10:1942489064

ISBN-13: 978-1-942489-06-1

Published by SkillBites LLC

First Printing, 2015

Printed in the United States of America

TABLE OF CONTENTS

PREFACE

It seems that every family has a "saver"– a collector of sentimental memorabilia who keeps the bits and pieces of family life and history stored away somewhere in a box.

In my family, that was my grandmother, Mary Barness. Apparently I inherited her passion for saving and for keeping track of the family lore. I have lots and lots of family photos, and I have enjoyed having them framed and displayed in my various homes over the years. But shortly before she died in 1986, my grandmother gave me several cartons that contained letters from both of her sons during their college years and World War II. I always intended to do something with these letters, but they stayed in the cartons while I lived in one home for 26 years, and then came with me when I moved several more times. The boxes always remained closed.

As I was getting ready to move yet again, I happened upon the boxes of letters once more. This time, I opened them and took inventory– there were easily several thousand, including close to one thousand from my Dad himself. The others were from my Uncle Lewis, my dad's older brother, and at first I intended to read his too after I had read those from my dad. But the task was just too daunting, so I finally boxed up Uncle Lew's letters and sent them off to another keeper of the lore, Lewis's oldest child, my cousin Carol.

I then set upon the task of reading the letters by my father, Herbert Barness. I wanted to organize them in a way that would be interesting and easy to read. The hardest part, of course, was deciding what to include. Some of the letters were from a country boy who had gone off to college and was away from home for the very first time. Some were from a college boy who went all the way to the South Pacific during World War II, and, thankfully, some were from that very same boy when he finally returned home.

As I read these letters, which follow him from age 14 to 25, it was amazing to see that the boy in them was also the man I knew as an adult: family-oriented, patriotic, optimistic, entrepreneurial, a leader, a natural politician, and a lover of sports and candy. It was such fun to discover where my dad's lifelong practice of swimming started, and to realize that his love of radishes, "skunions," Jell-O, and pineapples all had a long history before I had ever known him.

As I read the letters, I separated them into three piles: 1) "weather letters"– or letters that mainly talked about the weather and ordinary life; 2) letters of some interest to others, that revealed something personal about my father, his family, his community or the world; and 3) letters of great interest which painted a broader picture of the times, with notable personal, family, community, and world events as the focus. It is this last group of letters that I have included here. The letters are all dated, and almost all of them have been saved with their original envelope, including the stamp and postmark. And almost all were hand-written. The number of letters– and the frequency with which my father wrote– is staggering, as you will see. And remember, this is only a selection of the letters that my grandmother had saved.

My Dad shared some of the stories from this period in his life with my sister Nancy and me. We heard about walking to his one-room schoolhouse, and about the boat that he built in the family's basement. But our father never really wanted to talk about the war, although it was obviously one of the major formative experiences of his life. Looking back, most of his war stories actually revolved around Moke and Molly. I won't tell you any more (it would be too much of a spoiler!), so you will just have to read the letters for yourself.

I am 65 years old, and neither of my children is a saver (to say the least!). But these letters are treasures to me. All of us tend to think of our parents as we've always known them– as fully formed individuals– and only rarely do we get a glimpse of them as children and young adults. These letters are a legacy for the generations that come after my dad. Although he passed away in 1998, he was and will always be an enormous presence in our lives, and I want to make sure that my sister, my children and hers, and our grandchildren, have a chance to know this man– whom they may or may not have met– as he was in his youth. The stories from his later life live on, and these letters shed light on how they began.

I hope you enjoy reading these letters and meeting a boy as he became a man as much as I have.

—*Lynda Barness*

INTRODUCTION

Herb Barness wrote a letter to his grandchildren Jennifer, Melissa, Julie and Elizabeth in 1989, describing his early life. I found it recently and felt that it truly sets the stage for the letters in this book. Since the rest of the book is in his own words, it seems only fitting that the introduction is too.

1989
Warrington, PA

Dear Jennifer, Melissa, Julie and Elizabeth,

I was born in Philadelphia, Pennsylvania, on December 1, 1923.

My parents were immigrants who were married on October 24, 1920. My father came to this country at the age of 14, by himself. More difficult to believe is the fact that my mother came to this country at the age of 10—by herself—to join her father who had come to the United States two years before. She arrived in the United States in 1903. They met in 1919, were married in 1920 and had a son, Lewis, in July of 1921.

In April of 1924, shortly after I was born, my parents moved to Warrington, Bucks County, Pennsylvania from Philadelphia. They bought a farm of 98 acres on Bristol Road for $5000. That was a lot of money in 1924 so they had a mortgage on the farm because they did not have $5000. They worked on the farm and my father was really a farmer. At that time, Bristol Road was just a mud road and there was no electricity or any improvements on the farm. Because of this my mother had to boil water or heat water on a big old stove that burned wood or coal and then would pour the hot water, together with some cooler water, in the tub so that we could bathe or get washed. There was a well and a hand pump outside that we would use to pump water into buckets and carry the buckets of water into the house. In the wintertime it was very, very cold, but the water in the well did not freeze because it was much below the surface of the ground. They were certainly very difficult times for our parents, but they made sure we really never knew of many of the difficulties.

There were a few children within a mile or two with whom we could play, but for the first 8 or 9 years of my life, we really did not see many other children other than relatives who would come to visit us (or we could go to visit them).

The school we attended for the first 8 grades was about two miles from our home, and of course we walked to and from school every day. There was no such thing as school buses and very few people had automobiles. School had one big room in it with a potbelly stove in the middle of the room. There were two outhouses, one for the girls and one for the boys if we had to use bathroom facilities. I can remember in the wintertime, the schoolroom was very cold and we always wore sweaters and jackets during the school day. In the one room there were 8 grades, with only one teacher for all 8 grades. As a result, if we were interested, we could listen to her teaching all the subjects in every grade. As you know, my brother (your Great Uncle Lewis) went from 1st grade to 3rd grade to 5th grade, because when he got into 2nd grade or 4th grade he already knew all the questions and all the answers.

When I was 8 years old, my parents sold their farm and we moved to Easton Road, which is also known as Route 611. We moved there because by that time my father was trying to make a living selling real estate rather than farming and there was more automobile traffic on Route 611, which was a paved road, than there was on Bristol Road. Being an immigrant, my father spoke Russian and Polish very fluently. He was selling farms then to other immigrants who came from Russia and Poland because he could speak to them very well. When we moved to the house on Easton Highway [also called Easton Road, but it really was the major highway in the area], we had electricity and all the other conveniences that we take for granted today. Of course, we did not have television but we did have radios; we did not have refrigerators but we had iceboxes. The ice man would come several times a week and bring big blocks of ice which would be put into the top of the ice box so that the cold from the ice would go through the box and keep everything relatively cold. Of course in the summertime he had to come more often than the wintertime, and in the wintertime frequently we would just go outside and get some ice and bring it and put it into the box.

I started high school in 1936 in Doylestown, Pennsylvania. The high school was 4 miles from our home, so we either had to take a bus or get a ride to and from school by hitch-hiking or sometimes with a friend or our father. There still was no such thing as a school bus, but rather we went on the Philadelphia Rapid Transit Bus, which is now SEPTA. It cost 10 cents to go to Doylestown and 10 cents to return. Almost all kinds of candy was only 1 cent; ice cream cones, as well as Coca-Cola and other types of junk food, were 5 cents. In Doylestown, there was a Woolworth's "5 and 10 cent" store and other stores, which we really were not accustomed to, having lived in Warrington. There was even a movie house in Doylestown, so once a week my parents would take us to the movies. For my mother, father, brother, and myself to go to the movies cost a total of $1.

In the summertime we always worked in the garden to raise vegetables for the summer and try to keep them also for the winter. Very occasionally we would go swimming in a pond that was also used for the cows and other animals. We had no swimming pools in our area, but there was a swimming pool in Doylestown that we used after we started high school. For us a long trip would be to go into Philadelphia with our parents, and once every few years we might even go to New York to visit some other relatives. Money was very scarce in those days, but we ate well and we were always properly clothed. I suppose we ate well because we lived on a farm and grew almost all of our own vegetables and fruits. We even raised our own chickens and cows, so we had plenty of eggs and plenty of milk.

One of my teachers in High School– a Mr. Mike Beshel– who taught math, was responsible for me going to college. I went to a small high school where my brother was an outstanding student, and it was difficult for me to follow. However, Mr. Beshel insisted that I had the ability, and he personally took me to Bucknell University where I registered that very day.

In 1940, I graduated from high school, and for the first time in my life, I left home without my parents or brother. I entered college at Bucknell University, which created an entirely new atmosphere for me. I was studying engineering, and although I was not a particularly great student, I was doing fairly well. On December 7, 1941, America entered World War II, and at that time I was too young to go into the Armed Forces. However, on December 7, 1942, I enlisted in the Army Air Forces and was called to active duty two weeks later. I came home for the Christmas holidays, and then my parents took me to Harrisburg to get on a train, where we left for Florida, and my military career started.

I was placed into a school to study meteorology and graduated as a meteorologist from the University of Illinois in 1943. While in the Army, we were required to go to school from 8 a.m. to 9 p.m. because an emergency existed. That is why they took my 2 ½ years that I attended Bucknell University and, with the accelerated program in the Army, they gave me a degree. I then worked as a meteorologist for approximately six months, and since I had some previous engineering education, I had applied for some schooling in electronics and communications. After six weeks of this accelerated course, I was shipped to the Pacific, where I spent almost three years as an officer in the Army Air Force. My last position in the Air Force was as a Squadron Commander, headquartered on the island of Guam. I then returned home in 1946 and re-enrolled in Bucknell University, where I had started to get my degree in 1940.

I met your Grandmother, Irma Shorin, shortly after I returned to Bucknell, where she was also a student. I graduated in February of 1948, and we were married after she graduated, in June of 1948.

Love,

Popee

CHAPTER 1

1938-1940

WARRINGTON, PA

These letters were exchanged between my father Herb, while he lived with his parents in Warrington, PA and attended High School in the neighboring town of Doylestown, PA, and his older brother Lewis, who was a student at Harvard University. Herb was 14 years old and Lew was 17.

The envelopes from this period were addressed to Name, Town, County, and State but did not include street names. The postage was a 2-cent stamp.

In 1940, the postage went up to 3 cents for a letter.

March 26, 1938

Dear Herb,

I am very glad to learn that you are improving, at least becoming someone who does not turn people away. Congratulations!

Mike just sent me a letter, and told me that you are an assistant manager. More congratulations!

Are you going to speak at all this year? How did the teams make out at Allentown? How's the coach?

You're in so many activities: debating, baseball, declamation (?) news, etc., but how are your marks? Although they are unimportant so far as indicating education, you need them, unfortunately perhaps, to get into college.

Have you been thinking about what you intend to study?

Will see you soon.

Lewis

P.S. Will bring glove home.

October 8, 1938

Dear Lubitchka (etc.), [Lewis]

I will try to answer your letters more often.

We are all O.K. and making out O.K.

Just because Brown has a damn good team and Harvard, as usual, has a lousy one is no excuse for not going to the games. Why just look at D.H.S. [Doylestown High School], we lost our first game to Sell-Perk– 6-0, and then for a change we lost our second game to Ambler– 6-0, that is all the more reason why I like to go to the games—to support the team, and yell like 'l for em.

I, as you did, will answer your questions in order:

Dad sold the bungalow to Mr. Bowers' customer. It wasn't the man Dad expected. We came home about 7 p.m. and the same people that Mr. Bowers saw came about 8 p.m. the same night, and then came the next day to close the deal.

Dad sold the ground between Hutchinson's and Farber's old place, and on this he is building only a chicken house for Samuel H. Chambers, the teacher of the deaf in Philadelphia.

Miss Hoffman, Dad is expecting next week.

Dad did not go in to see Joe yet. Mother and I are O.K.

You shiftless skunk, Dad let me drive because he says I have to learn how to keep to the right side of the road some day!!! (I was not offended by your remark in the most).

I am studying, but am not overworking myself, and I really like school because I am having it easy.

Please do not answer the following sentence: when we came home Monday, and I stayed home Tuesday, when I got back to school Wednesday, we had an algebra test the first period and I got a 40. (Dad doesn't know it).

I'm glad you stopped sermonizing.

I don't know what college I'm going to, and I don't know what I want to be !??!!?

If you want to know how Beshel likes me, ask him, but how I like him I may answer thus: He doesn't let me teach him so very well! (I like him swell, but I hope I have a little favoritism).

I could use some assistance in Physics, but I'm getting along O.K., and I like the teacher Mr. Wertenberger. In two tests, in Physics, so far I've gotten an A+ and a B-.

I am in the Debating Club and I do think I will be a speaker, the topic is: "Resolved that the USA should join an alliance with Great Britain."

I am definitely on the negative side. (If you know anything about it, please write me.)

I am writing for the '"News" and I expect to be editor soon. I'll tell you details when I see you.

I tried out for the Harlequin play, "Pride and Prejudice," but I did not make it. (I was sort of disappointed).

I got a club ticket when you were home yet, and I've see 1 football game, that with Ambler.

If you aren't kidding about having a swell time in college, I think I have definitely made up my mind to go!

Dad sold another place (I think) to some very nice German people, but he will tell you about that.

Now I will start asking questions: DO you eat, and where. Do you like it better up there this year, and why. Why don't you go to the games (6 reasons). How do you like your room, and why. What should I take up, and why. Your decision is final.

Why don't you write to me oftener.

Are you lonesome, and why or why not.

Have you gone to the movies, and why not.

Do you have far to walk to classes. And where do you spend most time, in classes, studying, or Radcliffe. (Is it a 3-minute walk if you run to Radcliffe).

Well Harvard took it on the "chin'" again today 20-0, (ha-ha).

The 24th of this month is Mother's and Dad's anniversary, and I will do the buying this year. We will get them a small table and lamp for the living room and a small lamp for over the center of their bedroom (if it's O.K. with you!)

I like English best of all my subjects and I get my best marks in it too. (Miss Lehman—oo-la, la.)

Nothing else I can write because I don't have much ink left in my pen, but I am expecting a letter from you within 3 days.

Love from all,

Herbitchka

November 9, 1938

Dear Lou,

How are you? We received your letter tonight. What is the answer to the joke?

James is Governor!!!

Dad had several good prospects this week. I sold 30 tickets for the Harlequin play. I expect to get my pin this year.

I might send away for my license in about 7 weeks????

Beshel spoke to me about you today. He wanted to know if you're still home- sick??

Nothin much new. Saffiers [his cousins] got a cow.

Dad didn't paint the sign yet.

8 houses going up on Park Avenue, more expected, for Fox Farm.

No school Friday afternoon!!!

I am going to clean out the old car Saturday so we can get rid of it.

Sent away for '37 Chev. License. ¾ H.P motor for saw.

Love from all,
Herb

Dec. 1, 1938 [Herb's 15th birthday]

Dear Lou,

Today I am a man! I received your letter yesterday!

You talk about snow. You don't know what snow is! You don't have to shovel a 200-foot drive, 3 walks, 3 porches, a terrace, a garage (windows open).

For the first time this week, the men worked. We seem to be getting rid of most of our whiteness, although several feet still remain.

To tell the truth about school, I care less and less for it every day. In fact I don't give a damn any more. Today, I did or died in Algebra–we had a test--- ugh--- I think I did.

I don't know whether you knew it or not, but I expect to be a sailor or a soldier–probably neither.

I don't know what I want to be, and it doesn't worry me. Maybe I won't go to college. I can't decide on anything.

If there is still snow by Saturday, I think I'll try to go skiing?

I am trying out for the debating team tomorrow. Lansdale beat us 12-0. We won two games. Basketball will soon start.

Love,

Herb

December 19, 1938

Dear Lou,

We received your letter today, and we did get your receipt.

The weather is rather fair, but I'm afraid it's going to be storming by Thursday (report cards).

Last night, I went to Looges to get some bread, and I took a chance on a punch-board for 5 cents, and won a 1 lb., or less, box of candy. Today I took a chance from Mary Fox, and won a 5 lb. box of candy. I paid 9 cents for the chance.

Dad and Mother went to a refugee meeting last night in Bristol. (Dad gave $25). We will probably to go the movies tonight to see the "Great Waltz."

See you soon,

Love from all,

Herb

January 6, 1939

Dear Lou,

When you got back was Harvard still there?

Dad doesn't know about the report, so please don't write about it!

We are all fine and the temperature today was 65 above.

I suppose you want to know what I am doing in school?! I'll write you about it when I feel like but please don't write home about schooling!!!

Things are going O.K. so far, I am improving in Physics, have a History test next Wednesday or Thursday. Same way in all other subjects.

The road supervisor, Mr. Reilly, was here last night, and he said that we might have a building ordinance in Warrington.

Nothing else to say except that you forgot your pen (which I am writing with).

Love from all,
Herb

P.S. Did you see the new 50-cent piece? (Answer on the other side)
Neither did I, but I have her address!

January 9, 1939

Dear Lou,

We received a letter from you today, telling of all your happenings! You don't have anything on us, because we're having quite a hot time.

First of all, I got pinched!! Old Man Dollinger squealed on me, (the cop told me so) and I was stopped. I don't know the fellow, but all he did was tell me to get a license for my sake. (Don't write back about any of this stuff). This happened on Saturday.

Yesterday, we took another chip off the car. Dad was out with some people, and he left his car on Park Road. When he came back with the same people, the man driving hit the front fender on the driver's side, cut the tire, and broke the hubcap. Jess fixed the tire, and I suppose we'll get the rest fixed.

I spent an hour with Beshel today, and he helped me quite a bit.

As far as I know, we have a history test Wednesday– and an Algebra and Physics test sometime soon.

How is your cold?

Love,

Herb

PLEASE DON'T WRITE ANYTHING ABOUT SCHOOL.

We won a basketball game Friday and have another Tuesday!

February 12, 1939

Dear Lou,

How are you? We are all O.K., and the Gayls, Sunshines, and 2 Caplans [all cousins] are here. (Len and Uncle Morris are to a banquet). Booey and Ronney [cousins] are going to be married at Leonard's Bar Mitzvah (or in other words April 1.)

I received $1.19 for pictures I sold! I hope you don't mind but I'm saving this money to buy a jacket. If you want half, write, and I'll send it to you!

We came in 3 a.m. this morning from Orleans!

We have had some damn nice weather here, lately.

There isn't much news here otherwise.

Love from all,

Herb

February 19, 1939

Dear Lou,

The downtown gang was here today, and so were Aunt Eva and the kids.

Dad sold Witts the first place on Park Road. I made the agreement, made four new ones for Painters, and have to make the applications for Painters! I straightened out the office yesterday, by taking out all the cards from under the glass and putting in pictures of different houses. Mr. Beardsley took some pictures of Painters today, but Dad doesn't want me to develop them.

We are having swell weather here, the tractor was fixed, and I'm not sure but I think Dad expects to get a new truck soon, because he just had some more trouble with it. If you have time you can send Dorothy a get-well card– she is sick, but not very badly!

Mr. Beshel was here yesterday, and he wants to tutor me, but he does not want anyone to know about it! <u>I passed my first Algebra test this year!</u> I'll tell you how it happened: we had a test Friday morning with five problems and we were only to do four. I tried the first four, but didn't even try the fifth because I knew I couldn't do it. I got three right, thereby giving me a 75. I believe I'll be able to go out for baseball!!

Mother and Dad saw "Zaza" and "Jesse James" this week– I saw "Jesse James"– I liked it fairly well, and Mother and Dad liked it better than "Zaza."

I suppose you know that there is going to be a P.T.A affair here, Friday?

Well, I've told you all the news, now I'll ask you a few questions:

Where is your enlarger??

Did you see "Gunga Din"??

Are you still homesick??

Did you have any tests lately??

Have you gone out anyplace?

Do you still live in Radcliffe??

Nothing else new,
Love from all,
Herb

May 7, 1939

Dear Lou,

Well, we are having absolutely beautiful weather here, and it seems as though it is Spring. A few more signs of Spring are: The grass is growing and I have to cut it, and second– I got Spring fever and just when I have to study– I can't!!! I'm really in a bad way!

I bought a swell card for Mother and I am going to get her a $2.00 box of candy. She wants a house-coat which she is going to buy and I am to pay for that with the commission of selling Clark's a house on School Lane!

In case you haven't heard: I took those people out to look at the houses on Lower State Road, and then brought them back to the model home and spent some time with them there. Dad came, made an appointment with them, and closed the deal. They, like many, many other people, told Dad they thought I am very nice.

D.H.S. is in first place in the Baseball league, but we won't be there long!

Warrington is in the amateur Bux-Mont league and they won one and tied one. Dan Emerson pitches for the Republican Club in this same league, and he shut out Point Pleasant by a score of 12-0. He pitched swell ball, and he set some sort of record for this league.

In this weather when I <u>ain't</u> go nothing to do- "I just sit and think," but most of the time I just sit----!!! (Ain't it the truth)

Well- nothing else to say.

Herb

P.S. "Great men die young, and I feel sick already."!!!

WOW!!!!!

September 27, 1939

This letter is to Lewis Barness, who is now living in Adams F-32 at Harvard, from Herb on Joseph Barness Realtor and Builder stationery. Herb wrote in "and Sons" after Joseph Barness. Then he wrote,

"Pres: Joseph Barness

Sales Manager and Sales Representative: L. Abraham Barness

Chief Contractor: Herbert Barness"

Dear Mr. Barness [Lewis]:

How is your health?? We are all right here except that I have my usual mental ailments.

I AM NOT typing this letter because I want to show you that I can type much better than you, but at present, it is sort of convenient because I happened to be sitting by the typewriter.

I am working just as hard as usual at school. Dad has finished two cellars on near the top of Foxes hill. Did you know Alvin Fox? These cellars were dug by Daniel G. Martin.

Enclosed find the stuff that you did not want sent up, but asked for, anyhow.

Also find within the advertisements of some darn stationery.

Last Friday we had the first lesson of Health (in the book) and Wolfe called on me. I told him I didn't know the answer, so he said I get an "x". But as far as I am concerned about Wolfe, he can go to ~~Hell~~ heck. (I don't cuss no mo')

See you at the Harvard-Yale game,

Love from all to all,

Sincerely yours,

Herbert Barness, esq. per H. Chief Contractor

October 7, 1939

Dear Lewis,

How are you??

D.H.S. had a game today!

I didn't go to the game!

If you didn't send a card to Garges [neighbor] yet, please don't do so, because Mom thinks it isn't proper for you to do so.

I, by myself, took our trunk up to Hayman Radcliff to get it greased and oiled!

I am business Mgr. of the play!!!!!

I have husked my corn and I got an average crop. I'll send you some as soon as it dries!!!

Albie Cornell sent me a card, and I returned him a letter.

Dec. 1 is only 55 days away. [Herb's birthday]

Love from all,

Herbert Barness

P.S. Remember the World's Fair, yet?

November 3, 1939

Dear Lou,

I suppose miracles will never cease! Imagine receiving 2 letters from you in one week??? What's this world coming to!??? However, I will be expecting at least 1 letter a week from you since you are getting ambitious!

Dad and Mr. Bowers are in Phila. tonight seeing some people. Zada [Herb's maternal grandfather] came here today by bus, and the Western Glazing-A.J. Sunshine [cousin] Glass Companies have merged.

As to my R.C.…. It ain't important enough to talk about. I am, as I said, disappointed but I am also discouraged, and I am sort of failing!

We will start clipping your coupons for you.

Nothing else new,
Herb.

P.S. I am going to write to Albie right now and I don't feel like writing, but I will write you more later.

P.P.S. I have decided that this earth is a hell of a place to live in, but what can you do, no one has gotten out of here alive!!

P.P.P. S. Joke!!!

November 1939 (undated)

Dear Lou,

How are you? Mom and Pop went to Brabinders and all the Silversteins [relatives] were here, before.

The play was a swell success because we made about $300-$350 profit!!! (thanx to the business mgr.)

D.H.S. lost to Hatboro 14-1!

I got a new suit last night before the play!

I do believe that Warrington knows that you got 103 in a chem exam.

I am expecting a watch for my birthday, and I do mean you! P.S. Dad said he'd get me one if my marks were up.

I was again rendering my services to the Barness Construction Company, last Saturday, after a very brief absence. Dad had to hire 4 men in my place !! (when I was absent).

Weiland and Lou Adams are the 2 left of the 4, because Dad gave Keys a temporary vacation to Christmas and the other guy a permanent one. However, Blythe is working (or putting in time) with another man.

I have off this Thursday and Friday, and if you would like the have the honor of my presence, please write immediately!!! I would like to come, but I got me double.

Love from all,
Herb

December 8, 1939

On a postcard that says, Greetings from Warrington, PA, with a photo of a horse-drawn cart carrying hay.

Dear Lou,

Having a swell time. Wish you were here.

Love from all,
Herb

January 15, 1940

Dear Lou,

How are you and chemistry?

I, and we, received your letter!

Dad says that you should call whenever you want, only let us know ahead of time!

I sent away for an application to State and I am awaiting a reply. However, I expect to send applications to North Carolina, Dartmouth, and a few others, if possible.

I am getting along in school, but I am in a fog in respect to a college course. You mentioned research– What kind?

I will, undoubtedly, take a law course, but perhaps I may get interested in research! We will be able to talk more about it when you come home.

D.H.S won 2- lost 2- have a game tomorrow, and one Friday.

When are you coming home?

The snow was all washed away yesterday when it rained, and the men are beginning to work again.

Nothing else new,

Herb, The Mob

February 7, 1940

Dear Lou,

We received 2 of your letters! How are you?

We got 2 desks and they look ok.

Max hasn't come yet, but I suppose he'll be here pretty soon.

I am really and truly terribly busy because I have play practice from 7 to 9 every night; I have a P.O.D. book report to do; 3 English reports to write; and I have to make a stock chart– besides my other work.

I will send for catalogs to Cornell and Dartmouth- this Sat.

We are having beautiful weather, and the gang is beginning to come back.

I rang up an A- in a P.O.D. test and an A in an English "Macbeth" final.

Nothing else new,

Herb

February 20, 1940

Dear Lou,

I just received your letter (?).

In answer to your two questions, I can only say: I have not decided on a profession.

I was speaking to Mike [Beshel] about Bucknell, and of course he recommends it.

We are going to take a ride up to Bucknell to see the place, and this will probably be my destiny?

The snow is slowly melting, and the weather is clearing.

In reference to my D there isn't much to say. I don't deserve any more- that's all I guess.

As for Health, it can go to hell.

Mom and Pop are now reading your letter, which just arrived.

Nothing else new,

Herb

February 23, 1940

Dear Lou,

How are you? We received your letter today!

Mom sent you a package!

We still have one driveway closed, but it will be opened up tomorrow.

I got an application blank from Bucknell, and I think I'll be a victim at this school.

It's getting a little colder here now, and I think it'll freeze tonight!!

Well– nothing else to say,

Love from all,

Herb

March 12, 1940

Dear Lou,

You wrote some fighting words, and I'm just asking you to say them to my face!

I'm all better now, and will be in the play.

Dress rehearsal tonight– tomorrow night– matinee Thursday– skits Thursday night–and 2 performances (Fri. and Sat.)! I am in it both nights!

I am worn to a frazzle! However, I pulled in an A- in a P.O.D test.

I don't know Gertrude's name yet (Anna's baby) but when I find out definitely, I will write to you and tell you it is Gertrude Saffier. Anna [cousin] is very well, and you can send congrats.

We have been having beautiful weather, so I've decided to go out for Baseball next week.

When will you be home?

Albie is coming home next Wednesday.

Maybe we'll go up to Bucknell when you are home!

I think you better stop condemning Bucknell because that seems to be my destination!

Well– see you soon,

Herb "Janks"

April 18, 1940

On letterhead from The New Colonial Hotel, 15th and M Streets, Washington, D.C.

Dear Dad and Mother:

We arrived in Annapolis at about 12 today! I saw the most beautiful spectacle that could be possible for human men in uniform as they act as machines to the n'th degree. It was truly wonderful to see the men march as they did, and not one was out of step or moved any part of their body except when they had to!

I had a lousy lunch at Annapolis, but we had a chicken dinner for supper, and since I was fairly hungry, I enjoyed it but we couldn't use our hands on the chicken- so that sort of spoiled it.

We did some other touring today and we have a few more hard days of walking and riding ahead.

Love,

Herb

P.S. I forgot to mention that we arrived in Wash. at 5:30.

April 24, 1940

To Mr. Lewis Barness of Massachusetts:

Honorable Sir:

Received yours of the 21st and am happy to announce that I have taken care of your demands in this way:

First: I have already changed the weather because we have had 1 5/8 days of fair and warmer weather!

Second: The "Gayety" was terrible. The comedians were the only good part of the show. My fellow representatives and myself received about 5 hours sleep during our 4-day sojourn. (We didn't even go to bed the first 2 nights!!) The fellows were swell and we all had a wonderful time.

Third: The things that I can think of now that I enjoyed most are:

1 - FBI building. Saw all fingerprint files and guns and equipment of criminals and other stuff

2 - Supreme Court Building (beautiful)

3 - Lincoln Memorial (beautiful)

4 - Smithsonian Institute (wonderful)

Fifth: My complete apologies but I sent you one card from Annapolis and 2 cards from Washington. Perhaps you are using a different alias now, that's why you didn't receive them!

Sixth: Nothing new! My customers didn't come!

Seventh: I wanted to tell you about [cousin] Bernie but the mob told me to keep my mouf shut. However, he is <u>muchly</u> improved and will be home soon. Tanta Goldie [Herb's father's sister] is at Saffiers now.

Eight:	Last month	Now
Chemistry	D	C
French	C	C
Sales	C	D
P.O.D.	B	B
Health	EE	C
English Comp	B	C

Respectfully yours,
The Mob, Herb

July 6, 1940

Certificate of Admission for Mr. Herbert Isadore Barness, Warrington, Pennsylvania from Bucknell University.

On the basis of your certificate you have been accepted for admission to Bucknell University in the Freshman Class for the degree of Bachelor of Science in Commerce and Finance.

CHAPTER 2

1940-41

BUCKNELL UNIVERSITY

Herb arrived at Bucknell University in September of 1940, and immediately, the voice in his letters seems much more mature. Here, he writes to his parents.

Among the letters I read, there was a pile of cancelled checks, written on Doylestown Trust Company by Herb in 1940 and 1941. Most are written for $2 to $5 to pay for his living expenses.

October 31, 1940

Letter on letterhead from Herbert Barness, Box 13, Bucknell University, Lewisburg, PA.

Dear Mother and Dad,

First of all, I received your package this afternoon. It was part of what I asked for- but where was the chicken and baloney?

One of the other Jewish boys on this floor had a turkey brought up by his parents yesterday, and we all helped him get rid of it. He also had a salomia [salami?], but we left that for him. After seeing his baloney, it just made me more hungry.

If you can, will you please send me up 100 stamps. We can only buy ten stamps at a time here, and it's too much trouble always getting them.

It cost me $3 to join the American Society of Mechanical Engineers, but I think it's well worth it. In fact, they told me that I would be able to get a job in several aircraft factories for the summer. They told me this after I joined, so it wasn't only a sales talk.

I think I told you that I would like to go out for boxing. If I can possibly find the time, I am surely going to do this. Maybe if I get hit a couple of times, I'll want to quit

Enclosed you will find my Algebra test paper that I had on Tuesday. When I get my other marks, I'll let you know. However again, please do not think I am getting all A+, because if I ever get an A+ in Chemistry, I'll really feel happy. Please send all my other test papers back with the one I am enclosing because I shall need them very soon.

Love,

Herb

P.S. Have a chem test tomorrow.

P.P.S Bill for laundry for past two weeks: 91 cents

P.P.P.S. Tell Joe Gayl to write

P.P.P.P.S. Received a letter from Leonard, Lewis, and Sonny today

P.P.P.P.P.S. Freshman-Sophomore fight on Saturday.

Herb

November 7, 1940

Dear Mother and Dad:

Sorry I haven't written you sooner, but I just didn't have the ambition. However, I thought you'd probably be wondering what was the matter with me, so I decided to write.

There isn't any news here. School is going on as usual and the work is getting harder. I have a chem quiz tomorrow, and maybe a trig test also.

Well, I cut the first class so far this year. The electric current was shut off last night, and my clock did not go off.

I hated to cut the class, but I got up at 8:30, and I should have been in class by 8.

I was glad to hear that you sold the sample hoe, but how much did you give away with it. I read your ad in last Sunday's Inquirer, and if I know how you put ads in, I think you are pretty short of cash.

When I come home for Christmas, I think I'll draw a complete plan of outlay of Warrington. Putting all the streets to be built, and all the homes to be built in a good plan. Then Warrington might be a well-planned city. (I hope.)

Nothing else to write,

Love,

Herb

P.S. If I come home by train it will cost $6.40 round-trip to Phila. If I go by bus to Easton, it will cost $4.50 round-trip. How should I come home?

November 8, 1940

Dear Mother and Dad:

Well, I had a chem quiz this morning, but I don't know how I made out.

We got our trig test papers back, and I only got a B. We are having another trig test next week, and I hope to make out better.

You will probably get my mid-semester grades within the next two weeks. Don't be surprised if you see a few C's. I don't think you'll see anything lower than a C, and you won't find too many of them (I hope).

It's getting terribly cold up here. I wear a coat all the time.

I'm still expecting a package! If you haven't sent one yet, please don't forget a baloney, fried chicken, some of those Hershey miniatures, and any kind of cake. Donuts will be greatly appreciated. However, do not send up too much sweet stuff, because I am trying to keep away from it.

I have begun eating everything here, and I am gaining weight. Tomorrow afternoon I have to run three miles, to get in shape for boxing.

Well, it seems as though we still have the same President. As my Algebra teacher says: "Socialism is next in the USA." This is strictly a Republican school, and everybody hates the Democrats.

Well, no more news.

Love,

Herb

P.S. Has Booey sent me a shirt yet?

February 11, 1941

Dear Mother and Dad:

I received my pen and pencil set, and also your letter, today.

It isn't a question whether Lewis or I did better the first semester because Lewis is going to a different kind of school. I think in his freshman year he took four subjects, while I took eight. His four were probably just as hard as my eight. The only thing is that I had to get good marks if I wanted to go to MIT. I am making an application for there, so please send me my pictures immediately.

As I told you, I got my pen and pencil set, but where is the watch? And the radio? How about some goodies? You can send me up some fried chicken, a package of cakes, some homemade cookies, some halavah, and some candy. I could also use pretzels.

I have no more checks. I wrote my last check yesterday for $14. That makes about $24.98 that I have spent since I came back. I had to buy all new books, pay for my laundry, and get some extra equipment and supplies. Last semester, all my books and everything cost $73, this semester's cost about $22. $95 for books! Sometimes I wonder if it's worth it. It's an awful big investment.

Starting with next Monday (Feb. 17) I would like you to send me a check for three ($3) dollars. Then after next Monday send me $6 every two weeks. Please mail it so that I can have it by Monday. I have officially stopped my bank account, but I haven't written yet. Should I write, or will you tell them?

Well, no more news,

Love,

Herb

March 4, 1941

Dear Mother and Dad,

I received your letter today. I believe it was the longest letter I have received from you yet.

I accept the job with the Barness Construction Company. I'll draw the plans, hire the men, and build houses for less than you.

As for my mechanical drawing, I am getting it much better this semester. So far, I am ahead of the rest of the class, and I intend to stay that way. In fact, I have high hopes of getting a B out of the course if I do a little work.

I didn't intend applying to Lehigh and Drexel, but now I think I will. You told me about it, and I got a letter from Eugene Kline asking me why I haven't sent in my application. Next weekend I am going to send my applications. [I have no idea why he was applying to other schools!]

I don't think I'll come home this month because I will be home in April. It is only about 30 days so I won't bother. I could easily come home, but it wouldn't be worth it.

Well, that's all,

Love,

Herb

March 14, 1941

Dear Mother and Dad,

How are you? How is the weather back home? We still have plenty of snow, but it is melting fast. At least while you aren't able to do any work I am getting some mail every day. I received your third consecutive letter today.

By the way, I am going to send my laundry home next week. Keep all the clothes I send until I come home. In the laundry case please send me back the following:

one baloney

one fried chicken

some of those chocolate cookies

my brown-faced ping-pong paddle- I want the paddle because I am going to enter a tournament! Pick out the better of the two brown-faced rubber paddles.

Also in the case send up three cartons of cigarettes. Either Chesterfield or Philip Morris. No, I don't smoke, but since I didn't give the counselor or janitors any Christmas present, I think I will get them this small gift now and then give them a few dollars at the end of the year. Please send these three cartons up with the package because I know they will appreciate this gift more than a lot of other things.

Well, that's all the news here,

Love,

Herb

P.S. I will write more tomorrow

P.P.S. I have an English mid-semester tomorrow

P.P.P.S. Send up the package as soon as you get my case (if you can)

April 20, 1941

Dear Mother and Dad:

How are you? I received a letter yesterday, and one today, from you. I also received my laundry today.

I went downtown today to get a pair of shoes. I bought a pair for $4.00. They are brown and white. Don't forget to send me a pair of pants.

How is the weather back home? It was 95 degrees here! I went to watch a track meet this afternoon. We lost 72-55.

All the fellows have gone out beering tonight, but since I don't drink, I didn't want to go. I am the only one on the floor now. I have been studying, but now I am going to bed.

By the way, finals are only four weeks off!!! I hope I can pull some good grades. I don't expect any D's this semester, but I don't think I'll get any A's.

No more,

Love,

Herb

P.S. Please send me some 1-cent stamps

April 22, 1941

Dear Mother and Dad,

How are you? How is the weather back home?

One of the fellows in my Chemistry class told me that a picture of one of your houses was in the Record. Did you have many lookers? How many did you sell??

I am now going through my last five weeks of my first year in college! The time has gone by very fast. Somehow, I can't picture the thought of spending so much and yet so little time here.

I am a year older now, and if college has done for me what it should, I should be much smarter. However, I don't feel any smarter, although I do feel older.

By the way, have you:

Put in the flagpole??

Built a tennis court??

Has Sonny come back yet? How is Al Krout!

Well, I must write to Lewis now,

Love,

Herb

April 27, 1941

Dear Mother and Dad,

How are you? What's new back home?

I went to an auction sale today with all the fellows. Maybe I shouldn't have gone because I bought something. However, you can't yell at me for buying this because I bought two antiques for mother. I hope you will like them, mom. I am very positive they are antiques because I priced them at an antique shop and he offered me much more than I paid for them. In fact, I could have made about $71! The reason they are so valuable is because they both were used in the Revolutionary War (1776) and the people that owned them have a story about them. One of the things is a gun. It is a four-foot muzzle-loader with a bayonet (a long knife) on the end. It's the kind of gun you see in the pictures about the wars of old. [My note: Oh, no! I had no idea. I had that musket and gave it away when I moved from my house to an apartment!!]

The other thing is a candle maker. It was also used in the war. I don't believe you have any antiques as old as these.

Well, my school-work is improving because I am working. In four weeks, our finals begin. I hope these are my last four weeks at B.U.

That's all,

Love,

Herb

P.S. I will keep the antiques up here until the end of the year. They cost very little for the actual worth of them. However, I'm afraid I will soon need money because I need glasses badly.

May 2, 1941

Dear Mother and Dad,

I received your letter yesterday. It was almost time that you wrote. You know, you have to write letters in order to receive them! However, I realize you must be busy, but you once told me I could never be too busy to write!

Well, I hope your season has started! Sell about six more places before I come home, so that I can have sometime to work on. This is going to be our big year– with me building and you and Lewis selling??

I had a chem quiz this morning. I think I got a 100 in it. I am starting to work a little now, but the weather is too nice.

I am really hitting my stride in drawing. I had to take apart a double emery wheel, and draw each part of it separately. This is just the kind of stuff I like to do, so I made out pretty well in it.

By the way, do you have any loose cash? If you do, I would like to have some as soon as possible because I have to change glasses. I am very low on the financial side. If you can will you please send me some cash, or else deposit some money to my account, and send me a checkbook. I think there is a checkbook in my sock-drawer. I won't need much because I only have four more weeks here, but the sooner you can give me some, the better it will be.

Is Marion [cousin] still home? How is she? How is everybody else? How are they at Saffiers? Does Dorothy still "put in time" on the piano?

It will be all right if you don't come up here for Mother's Day because I will catch up on some work then. However, you absolutely must come up around June 5th.

Well, that's all,

Love,

Herb

September 23, 1941

Dear Mother and Dad,

I have been here for 9 days, and today was the first time I received a letter! You may be busy all day long, but at night you have some free time! Up here I have classes from 8 a.m. to 5:30 p.m. every day! Then from 6 p.m. to midnight I have to study!!

Besides your having more time than I– you are not living by yourself. There are two of you at home, and only one of me up here. Therefore you should write me twice as many letters. Also since you have more free time, you should write me two more extra letters. To put it in good English: I should receive four (4) letters to your one!!!

Well, enough of that. It is all settled that I should receive 4 times as many letters as you.

Now to get down to business! Did you buy the farm yet? Did you start to build the hosiery mill? Did you buy a concrete mixer? Are the two houses on Quimby's sold yet? Also how about the one next to Igoes'?

Have you hired any new men? Have you fired any, or has anybody quit? Don't forget I gave you the responsibility of finishing my tennis court!

How is "Billie"? Has he been killed yet? Tell him I was asking for him!!

Please let me know who you are going to bring up with you for Father's Day. I have to make reservations for the rooms very shortly. I will write to Duncan, and also to Clarance to find out ho much I owe him.

If there will be six of you coming up I will have to get three rooms. If you want to bring up Leonard or Harriet [cousins around his age] also let me know.

Well, it's about time you sent me up a package. I want my extension cord, chocolate drop cookies, etc.

Nothing else now,

Love to all,

Herb

OS. Since this letter is four pages long, and your letters are only one page- you owe me 4 x 4 or 16 letters.

October 17, 1941

Dear Mother and Dad,

Although I just spoke to you, I found that three minutes is not long enough to tell you what I would like to tell you.

First of all, I believe it is self-evident that I hope you are not too affected by the death of one so dear as a mother. Everyone will probably say she is better off now, but that doesn't count. We all like to believe that nothing is as good as life itself, yet in this case it wasn't hard to see that Buba [Herb's maternal grandmother] wasn't getting too much enjoyment out of living. Ever since I have known and remembered her, she was always being neglected by someone. But I rather not write any more about this because it brings back memories, and now it is too late to think of the past.

However, the main reason I am writing now is to ask you both to come up here for Father's Day. I know it may not seem proper to go out for enjoyment at a time like this, but there will be absolutely no gain in staying home. Although I usually say I am not homesick or lonely, I really do want you to come up here for Father's Day this year more than ever.

If Dad comes up by himself, no one will have as good a time and nothing will be gained. Therefore, since I want to see you both, I would like either both of you to come up here– or else neither. I am quite sure Dad will agree with me.

Must study now,

Love,

Herb

October 20, 1941

Dear Mother and Dad,

What's the matter– I haven't heard from you for over a week!! You know if you want to receive letters, you must write.

I happened to be looking at Harvard's football schedule, and I saw that Harvard plays Yale on November 22 at Harvard. I get off for Thanksgiving on the 19th, and since we expect to go up then, we might as well see the game– don't you think?

When are you going to let me know if you are coming up for Father's Day? I will have to make arrangements very soon.

I read your ad in the Inquirer yesterday. It was very attractive except for the price.

If you can find a nice farm– about 250-300 acres and not too expensive, pick it up for me. The fellow that came home with me and I have been talking about building our own aircraft factory. We have names picked out for the planes we will manufacture, and now we are working on the design of the factory. Just a dream– but one can never tell.

Well, I suppose you know that Harvard beat Dartmouth 7-0, and Bucknell beat Boston University 6-0. It rained during the whole game and I got a nice cold. Feeling ok now.

Nothing else to write,

Love,

Herb

October 23, 1941

Dear Mother and Dad,

I just received your long letter and lecture. This letter is definitely an answer to your letter.

But before I start answering your letter, let me explain my side of the case. First of all, I am being convinced that I am too young to be in college. I find that I do not have the mental powers that all of the older boys have. Perhaps some of my mental qualities are better than older boys, but when one is taking engineering, experience as well as brains counts. This isn't the experience of working, but experience that only age can give you.

Now you can say, "Look at Lewis– he was younger than you, and he made out very well in college." I agree with you. I have been hearing the story of "why can't I be like Lewis" ever since I can remember!! Lewis is just an exception. He works hard, and he gets good marks. He was brought up different than I. Whenever anything good was done– Lewis always did it. Lewis was always praised, he was smart, and he was always very serious. While you spent all your time praising Lewis and looking after him to see that he did well, I was left to do whatever I wanted to do. Your time was occupied with your work, your worries, and Lewis. Your worries consisted of your business and me.

Lewis was never a child. He was brought up as an adult. When he was ten years old, he could do many things that a 15 year-old child couldn't do! But—he never went out to play football, or baseball, or try to build things, or run around with the rest of the kids. He was in the house studying, while I was out playing. As a result, Lewis got A's and I got D's! And every time we got our marks, you always said, "why can't you be like Lewis."

In your letter that I just received, you said you wish I would get a little older and get more sense. I'll agree with you that I'm not very smart– In fact, I'm trying to tell you that I'm not smart. But the point is, ever since I got out of grammar school, you have been hoping that I get a little older and get some more sense. You keep telling me this because you are always comparing me with the sense that Lewis had!

Don't forget I am only 18 now. I am growing into manhood but I am always referred to as a kid. Perhaps if you met all the other 18 year-old boys here, you would not think I am still a child, and I do not have childish ideas.

The second point you made was about Mother coming out. I don't like to write about this because it will not make mother feel too good, but I will always say what I believe.

First of all, I think it would do Mother good to take the day off and come out. Secondly, it might give her a chance to forget the past. The third reason I think mother should come out is because I honestly see no reason for her, or any of the other sisters to remain in mourning. Although it is conventional to mourn for 30 days, why should anyone mourn the death of someone treated very badly. It isn't any secret– everyone knows that Buba wasn't even being treated like a human. I often said that if I ever got in Buba's condition, I would rather die. She was always talked to like a child, and no one had any deep affections for her. Therefore, to sum this up, I can make the statement: why mourn for someone after they are dead, but while they are alive treat them terribly.

Maybe I have the wrong idea, but I know if I ever treat anyone badly, I am not going to sympathize with them.

Now for your third point.

I don't know if you just don't want me to ever work for you, or if you just want to keep me in college. Whatever it is, I can tell you that if I ever quit or get kicked out of college, I won't come home to work, or even come home.

You said in your letter that I am wishing to get kicked out of school. As I told you before, I have classes five days a week from 8 a.m. until 5:30 p.m. Now if you think I stay up every night until one or two or three o'clock, just to get kicked out, you are fooling yourself. I can honestly say that if I flunk any subject here it will not be my fault. A person can work so much and no more. I need sleep so badly that I often can't think straight.

You are quite right, I don't like to take out customers. However, it isn't because I don't think I can talk to them, it is because I don't think people have faith in a salesman who is only 17 years old.

Now about the car. I know I can't have a car up here, but I can say I would like to have one. I realize I'm no playboy, but I wouldn't want a car to run around in. However, it is no use discussing this because it isn't important.

Well, now you can see how I feel about certain things. I hope you won't keep thinking whatever I do is like a kid.

Nothing else to say,

Love,

Herb

October 28, 1941

Dear Mother and Dad,

How are you? Is something wrong? Over the phone it sounded as if something was wrong!

Here is the list of what I would like you to bring up:

several shirts

clothes hangers

a woolen shirt if you can get me one

candy

potato chips

cake

chocolate cookies

<u>a nice big baloney</u>!

I would like to have 4- 8 ½ x 11 picture frames to hang up. I have some pictures of airplanes that I want to frame.

Be sure to mail me the card immediately, if you haven't already done so.

Nothing else, see you soon,

Love,

Herb

P.S. I also need stamps.

November 6, 1941

On the back of the envelope, Herb wrote "Warrington– known as "God's Country"

Dear Mom and Pop,

How are you? How is the weather back home?

Well, the baloney is gone, the potato chips are gone, and now the halavah and cookies are going. I think the rest of the stuff will last til next week, and then I'll be home in two weeks.

In Surveying Lab, we are now laying out a house. While we were doing this work I began to think of the instrument you have. I am afraid that yours isn't accurate enough to stake out a house, but it is good enough to find out if the house is level. Perhaps someday you will be able to get a better one.

Is Costa still working for you? Has he painted our house yet?

Well, from now until Thanksgiving I think I have a test every day.

No more news,

Love,

Herb

December 1, 1941

Dear Mother and Dad,

I am very sorry I couldn't have much of a conversation with you this morning, but at the time you called, it was the middle of the night to me.

Last night, myself and another fellow went over to the Engineering Building to do some work, and we said we wouldn't come back until we finish. So we were working constantly from 9 p.m. until 4 a.m. We got a lot of work done because we had to.

After you called, I went back to bed, and finally woke up at 2 o'clock.

I got a birthday card from Harriet today. I also got your letter in which you sound very disgusted with me. However, if you knew how much work I did last week, you wouldn't wonder why I didn't write.

It is true, I didn't have any picnic when I was home for Thanksgiving, but I was quite worried about my test and I don't think I could have had a good time. Also, if you knew how worried I was about the test I had last week, you wouldn't think I am very irresponsible!

I don't know what you think I do up here, but I can assure you that I'm not having a wonderful time.

You probably don't consider a C a very good mark, but if you will look up Lewis's record, you will see that he got a C in Physics when he was a sophomore in college. Anyhow, as long as I can get C's I 'll be satisfied.

Well, it's 12:30 now, and I still have an hour's work so I better sign off. I'm 18 now, and I hope you will be more satisfied in my future years than you were in my past.

Love,

Herb

December 2, 1941

Dear Mother and Dad,

I am just about ready to go to sleep now, and sleep for a few days.

Saturday, I went to bed at 4:30 a.m., Sunday at 3 a.m., and last night I didn't go to bed at all! I started working on some surveying, and descriptive geometry, at 7 p.m. last night. I finally finished about 7:30 this morning! I was working in the engineering building with three other fellows, and I didn't even come back this morning to change clothes, I just went straight to my two classes.

This afternoon I have a lab, and tonight I have to study for a calculus test. So I doubt if I will get any sleep for a long time.

I got a singing telegram from the Caplans this morning. The company called last night, but I wasn't here to receive it.

Our Christmas vacation starts the 20th, but I doubt very much if I will be home on that day. If I have any work to do, I am going to get it done before I leave for home.

No other news– we have a little bit of snow.

Love,

Herb

P.S. How is Billie?

P.P.S. Are you going to give a Christmas party for the men?

December 18, 1941

Herb received the following letter from the Department of National Defence Air Service, Ottawa, Canada:

Dear Sir:

Acknowledgement is made of your letter of December 1, in which you ask for information with regard to the procedure to be followed in making application for entry into the Royal Canadian Air Force.

For your convenience it has been arranged that all such enquiries may be handled in the United States. It would therefore be advisable for you to apply direct to the nearest branch of the Canadian Aviation Bureau as shown on the attached list. All information required will be forwarded you immediately.

It is hoped your desire to be of service will be gratified.

Yours truly,

H.P Crabb

Group Captain, for Chief of the Air Staff

CHAPTER 3

1942

BUCKNELL UNIVERSITY;
HEADING TO WAR

The year 1941 ended with the bombing of Pearl Harbor and the United States' entrance into World War II. Although Herb is still at Bucknell, the focus of his letters now shifts to the war and his efforts to join the Armed Forces.

January 15, 1942

Dear Mother and Dad,

Since I have been back at school, I have continued to write you at least once a day- and sometimes twice. Well, this letter will probably conclude my continual writing. With only one week to go, I am, and will be very very busy.

Saturday afternoon I am going to take the physical examination for the aviation branch of the Naval Reserve. If I pass, I will be in the Naval Reserve as an ensign. The same commission as if I went to Annapolis. They will let me finish college, paying part of my way through. Then, I will be an aviator in the Navy.

If I don't pass the physical exam, I can take it over again and again until I graduate from school.

Well, no more news.

Love,

Herb

January 17, 1942

Written Friday night

Dear Mother and Dad,

Tomorrow morning I take my physical examination for the Naval Reserve. If I pass I'll send you a telegram. If I fail, I'll write and tell you what part I failed.

Well, yesterday in Chapel, President Marts told us that it is compulsory for engineers to go straight through school until they graduate. This means that I will graduate (I hope) as a Mechanical Engineer in September 1943. In other words, I will be 19 years old when I graduate.

Our next vacation is from May 23 to June 8. On June 8 we start school again. Then we get off for Christmas– and then for graduation!!

Well, that's the latest news here,

Love,

Herb

January 17, 1942

Written Saturday, noon

Sticker on the back of this envelope says, V for Victory. Join the V Club of America

Dear Mother and Dad,

Well, I went to take my physical examination this morning! I started to take my exam when they noticed on my application that I was only 18. So, they told me they wouldn't examine me now– I should come back when I'm 20!! It looks as though I will have to get out of college and work a while before I can get in the air corps.

I received your package Thursday, and it was very good. Any time you feel like sending me some more, it's ok.

No other news,

Love,

Herb

January 19, 1942

Dear Mother and Dad,

It's a beautiful day in Lewisburg– but I have a slight cold– and I am too young for the Reserves!

After I found out about the air corps having the age limit, I signed up as an ambulance driver in case of an emergency here at Bucknell. I will be taking Military Training, and I will get 30 hours of instruction in driving. Also I (all sophomores) am required to take a complete course in first-aid.

Tell Harriet to buy the record called "Dear Mom" and you listen to the words of it. I think you will like it very much. All the fellows up here really think it's very good.

Well, no more news,

Love,

Herb

Don't forget the record!

[My note: I just had to google this, and here's what I found on Wikipedia:

Dear Mom was a 1941 World War II song with words and music by Maury Coleman Harris released by Republic Music Corp. The song was inspired by the 1940 Selective Service Act. The original recording was by Sammy Kaye and his Orchestra, with vocals by Allan Foster from the Victor Records stable. This was overshadowed by a recording in 1942 by Glenn Miller.

The lyrics take the form of a "Dear Mom" letter from a serviceman:

The weather today is cloudy and damp Your package arrived but was missing a stamp Your cake made a hit with all the boys in the camp How they loved it.]

February 17, 1942

Dear Mother and Dad,

Again I say I am sorry for not having written sooner, but again it can't be helped.

I received your letter this morning. Glad you sent the pictures, but where are the pictures of the planes?

I keep thinking of all the things I was going to do this summer if I came home, but I guess I'll never be able to do any of the things I used to do. For the next time I have vacation from school, it will be in 1943 when I graduate, and then my vacations will be over for a long time.

I was thinking of surveying all of Warrington, after I got my A in surveying, and drawing a large map of it. Also I thought I would work in a shop or factory to get some experience before I graduate. But now, I will be having the same routine for the next year and one-half, and then I will have to get settled, or else get in the Army. I think I will choose the Army.

By the way, although I don't want to remind you of my marks, if you can remember, the first semester of last year I got a <u>D</u> in Mechanical Drawing and I hated the course. The second semester, when the work got tougher, and I worked harder, I got a <u>C</u> in Mechanical Drawing. Then, this last semester, when I took the hardest drawing course, Descriptive Geometry, I got a <u>B</u>! However, this was a great surprise to me because I really thought I flunked this course.

Well, although I hate to settle down and get serious, I have to start because this work is getting me down. I enjoy all my courses very much (except Physics), but the profs say they want good engineers– or else none at all.

I like my new room very much. In fact the more I think of it, the more I like it. I still haven't received the rug or cot. Have you sent it yet? I am getting much more work done here than I used to (I think).

What's the Navy doing these days? Have they started working or preparing for anything? How is everything else in Warrington?

Love,

Herb

February 27, 1942

Dear Mother and Dad,

Received your letter this morning, and since I have some free time, I thought I might as well write.

First of all, I'll probably call next Monday night. The reason I never let you know that I will call is that I never know when I will call until I do call!

How are things at home? Any good prospects?

I received an announcement of Gene's [cousin] wedding yesterday. However, there was no invitation included. Not that I expect to go anyway, but don't they send out invitations? I also noticed that Leo's invitation was printed on much better paper than Gene's.

I don't believe I will send them a telegram because if I did they wouldn't want to read it in public. If it were in my power to declare that he is no longer my cousin, I would do just that. If I ever thought that my brother would ever get married to escape the draft, I surely would never even speak to him. Therefore, I shall never have the slightest regard for Gene. If I get an invitation for his wedding, I will write him a nice long letter telling him why I won't come and what I think of him. I sent Lewis a copy of a telegram I expected to send to Gene, but Lewis advised against my sending it.

The work is getting harder here each day and each week. I have two very important tests tomorrow that I must study for.

I received a letter from Harriet this morning in which she told me she got a job. She also said that Aunt Rae is sending me a box of Fannie Farmer candies. They are the kind of relatives I like to have!!

Well, no more to write,

Love,

Herb

March 11, 1942

Dear Mother and Dad,

Received your letter this afternoon. Glad to hear that Pete sold a place.

How is the weather back home? Are you able to go on with your work? This may be the last letter you will receive from me for several days because we are having a flood up here. All the buildings on the bottom of the hill are being emptied. By tomorrow noon they expect the water to be 13 ½ feet above the river. However, up on the hill everyone is calm, because we are too high to be affected. They are moving all the girls off the first floor of their dorms.

Well, I have definitely decided what I want to do when I get out of here. Now the next part you can do for me. Pull a few strings, become a friend of Grundy, or do anything else that's on the level to get me an appointment to Annapolis or West Point. As I have always told you, I think I would like a military life. Guffey and Davis are the two men in Pennsylvania who can get me into either of the two institutions. I hope you take me seriously because since I would be getting in the Army when I get out of school, I might as well get the best position I can. As far as expenses would be, the government pays each student to attend these schools. Yes, if you would like some honor and pleasure, as well as giving me a better start than 95% of the people in the USA, get me an appointment to West Point or Annapolis, and I will do the rest!

The thing is, you have to start working on it now, because it takes a year for an appointment to go through. Also, a student must be under 20 when he enters! This gives me a better chance than the better-than-average college student. Remember, these two schools are the most democratic institutions in the world, and there is no discrimination of any race, color or creed.

If you have the opportunity, please do whatever you can. However, Lewis wrote and told me you would probably be up in April when he comes home. So, until then, see if you can make a Captain out of me.

No more,

Love,

Herb

P.S. Will call Friday, March 13 between 7 and 8.

March 18, 1942

Dear Mother and Dad,

I did not write to you during the weekend, so I'll try to make this a nice long letter. If I can think of everything, this will have to be very long.

First of all, time #9999– we have no Easter vacation whatsoever. I had heard that we were to get Good Friday off, but one of the fellows went in to see the Dean and he said he didn't hear anything about it. After all, what is a vacation in the time of war. The soldiers, and sailors, and workers won't have a day of rest for a long time, so we are rather unimportant characters to ask for a vacation. Although I like it less than you do, I have done no complaining. I did hope to get home sometime this semester, but it will be almost impossible. There are only seven more weeks left anyhow, so it won't be too bad.

When I do come home, I will have three weeks off. In this time I expect to accomplish many things. First of all, I will need some clothes for the summer and fall. Then, probably for the last time, I would like to work on the jobs for about three days. Also, for the last time, I would like to either help grade a lawn or dig a cellar with the tractor. Since the government is asking everyone to do more farming, I suppose you too will grow a larger garden. At least, by the time I get home I hope the radishes and onions will be ready to eat. I know I'll miss the sugar corn, cucumbers, tomatoes, peppers, peas on the pod, carrots, and whatnot, but these things won't be too terrible. It's hard to realize, but for the next several years, I won't be home any more than if I were actually in battle. I'm not trying to be sentimental- because you know that's not my line, but things like these keep creeping around in my mind.

Now to tell you about West Point and Annapolis. I had written to the War Department in Washington for their bulletins, and I have received them. Each Senator and Congressman gets 5 appointments to Annapolis, and three appointments to West Point. This means that each Senator and House of Representatives member always may have their appointments filled.

If you know, or know someone who knows our Congressman or either Senator, I would like an appointment to West Point. I don't care for Annapolis too much, but if I couldn't get in West Point, I would gladly accept Annapolis. However, it should be relatively simple to go to West Point. If I can get an appointment, I will not have to take any examinations to enter because I will have four years of college. If you do not object to the idea of it, the only thing to do is try to get an appointment. I suppose you may not be too sure whether you would like me to go to West Point or not, but I think it will be very easy to convince you of it when I see you. I will not necessarily have to lead a military life after I get out, but if I want to then, I could do so.

Well, it's lunch time now, and since I have no more to write, I'll end,

Love,

Herb

P.S. You can send me a package anytime.

P.P.S. When you come up, please bring me a doily for my bureau- it's the same as my desk at home. Also would like to have "<u>Bartlett's</u> <u>Familiar</u> <u>Quotations</u>."

March 20, 1942

Dear Mother and Dad,

I have just come back from a conference with the head of the Mechanical Engineering department here.

I went over to see him to ask him what subjects we are going to take this summer, and also ask his advice about my entering the military academy. All he did was praise me for thinking about going to West Point. He said no one else had ever asked him about it, but he thought it was absolutely the smartest thing to do. He said when I graduated from there, I will be 22 years old and will probably have more experience and be a better man than any engineer that ever graduated from Bucknell. So if you don't mind, I have very very definitely decided what I would like to do.

You didn't "raise your son to be a soldier," and your son does not want to be a soldier for the rest of his life. With my engineering degree, my professor told me that the Army would absolutely give me a position as a technical engineer.

The only things that I need now are your consent– and an appointment. Whoever told you that only one from each state is appointed certainly does not know what he is talking about. I would send you the catalogues I received, but I will see you in two weeks.

Today, the students were taking up a petition to get Good Friday and Saturday off. If we got these two days off, I would come home Wednesday afternoon because I only have one class on Thursday. Although I want this vacation just as much, if not more, than the rest of the students, I would not sign the petition.

See you soon,

Love,

Herb

Remember– each Senator and Congressman has three appointments to West Point, and five to Annapolis!

March 21, 1942

The envelope is addressed to Dr. L.A Barness, but inside the letter says:

Dear Lou, Mother and Dad.

Sunday it snowed. Yesterday it was beautiful and all the snow melted. Today, it has been snowing since I got up (5:50 a.m- that's the time they get up at the Point) and we now have about one foot of snow.

It's easy to see who is more in demand in this country- engineers or doctors! They can give you quacks a week off, but we are too vital for defense (I hear it's going to be offense soon) so we must stay and work.

We get an official Easter vacation! Sounds good, yes? Well, since everyone was yelling about going to school on Good Friday, the school decided to give us a vacation. Her is what we get: No classes from Noon, Friday until 3 p.m., Friday!!! Three whole hours off!– But not for engineers– anyone having a lab must attend!!!!

I was thinking about knocking off this week and coming home, but I had a test this morning, and I have two more this week.

What good were your checks? Your name wasn't on them! I'll bring 'em back when I come home???

How is my appointment to West Point? Do I have one yet?

Since I am a major sleuth, I take it that you and Dad ate in Horn and Hardart's last night in Jenkintown. You said in your letter that you were going to Phila., and the letter was mailed 8 p.m. from Jenkintown. I received it 9 a.m. this morning.

Well, I guess I better go eat!

Herb

P.S. Work on that appointment! If you think I should see the guy from West Point or Mr. Masters, make an appointment with them! Thanx.

P.P.S. Will probably call some night and tell you when I am coming home..

P.P.P.S. Am not interested in relatives– am coming home to be home!

March 25, 1942

Dear Mother and Dad,

I just came back from two conferences with two mechanical engineering professors. The first one I went to see told me about aviation and West Point. The second one I went to see told me about engineering and West

Point. Perhaps you do not think it advisable for me to ask all my professors about West Point, but they are very glad to see that I come to them and it may mean a higher grade for me. I usually ask them a few questions, and then they tell me their life story.

Anyhow, two more check marks for West Point. Both men thought it a very very good idea to go to West Point or Annapolis. One advised me to finish here, the other told me to go as soon as possible.

I would like to talk to a graduate of West Point, but as I understand, anyone completing his course there would only have praise for it. As one of my profs said today: "If you graduate from West Point, you will be a well-rounded, informed engineer of fine character."

Unless Masters knows either senator, or the congressman from our district, I doubt if he can do anything for me.

Since I will see you next week, I will not write any more about West Point. However, the point is it takes almost a year to get an appointment.

Well, am feeling quite well today. Got several good marks in tests.

Love,

Herb

April 8, 1942

Dear Mother and Dad,

I have not received any mail from you yet.

Yesterday I paid a deposit on my room so that it will be reserved for this summer and next Fall. I paid a bill I had at the bookstore, and I got a belt and pair of suspenders. If I have time next week, I will get a pair of shoes. As the saying goes "baby needs a new pair of shoes," therefore you better make a few sales!

Did the settlement for the farm go through all right? Maybe we can explore those woods when I come home for vacation.

It seems to me as though I enjoyed this past weekend at home better than any other vacation I had since I have been here.

First of all it was good to get home. That alone was very nice, but this was the first time that I did not get yelled at. Perhaps what I have been hearing for the past 18 years has come true– I have grown up, and I'm not a child anymore. Maybe it's because of the war, maybe it's me, or maybe it's just the way it was at home, but I certainly enjoyed it. As I told you at home, I still think the outside of the house needs a painting, and although all the lumber, boilers, terra cotta, etc., are a sign of prosperity, I think you would look just as prosperous if they were in back of the garage.

This Friday I have two very difficult tests. Therefore I am going to start studying for them this afternoon.

Well I still want to go to West Point! Most of the fellows who are of age now are signing up with the Army or Navy Reserves. If possible I would like to have everything arranged so that when I come home for the three weeks, I can see all the necessary people.

Nothing else now,

Love,

Herb

April 9, 1942

Dear Mother and Dad,

I just received your letter in which you told me you saw Watson. I suppose he could fit it up, but couldn't he write to our congressman or senator immediately? Although he does not know me I think you might be able to tell him about me, or give him some references about me. I don't want to seem too persistent, but I won't be home for at least 5 weeks, and this is the time of year most of the students are looking for appointments.

Also, if you don't mind, and if you see Masters shortly, you could ask him to see what he can do. Perhaps he can arrange to get me an appointment with his connections. However, do whatever you this is best, but don't forget in 5 weeks a lot can happen. If you talk to anyone about this with any pull ask them if they, or you, think I should write to our congressman, well, enough for that.

Tomorrow I have two very difficult tests. I have been studying a little, but today and tonight I am really going to work.

Winter is here again! It started snowing last night and it hasn't stopped yet. This is really a snowfall too! It looks just like it did around Christmas time.

Glad to hear you are working ok. Now sell a few homes. I am going to try to get a counselor's job up here for the rest of my college course. If I get it, it means that I get my room free, and $100 off tuition! However if I do get it, I will be the first Jew to be a counselor, so I don't know how good my chances are.

No more to write.

Love,

Herb

May 16, 1942

Dear Mother and Dad,

I expect to call you tomorrow morning, so I will probably speak to you before you receive this.

As you already know, I am finished Wednesday, and start school on Monday. This only means 4 days off until July 3. In these four days I hope to get a lot accomplished. Mainly, I would like to find out about West Point.

As yet, I don't know how I'm coming home. I will probably take a train, and then come out by bus since I won't be carrying any baggage. I have neglected sending my laundry, but I will do so on Monday.

Two tests down, and two to go. If I make out as well on the next two as I think I did on the last two, I will be satisfied. However, my two tough ones are coming up.

Myself and another fellow have been invited to a professor's home for dinner tomorrow. This makes two different profs who seem to like me. If I ever need any reference from school to help me get into the Point I will have a very easy job getting them.

It has been a very miserable day up here today. We have had rain all day.

Glad to hear you can get gas, but I guess the rationing doesn't do business any good. How do your chances look for getting defense housing? I have my fingers crossed!

How is the garden coming along? One of the working men around the college has a garden right outside here. I keep telling him what a beautiful garden you have at home, so he told me that I could help myself to all the skunions and radishes that he has. I have helped, and instructed him with his garden. It makes me feel good to know a little about gardening. I can see now that I passed up many valuable things when I was home which I always neglected because I took it for granted that it didn't matter. There were also many things around the job which I passed up.

How are the flowers? Have you separated the tulips? Are they in bloom? How about all the others

Well, I'll find out everything when I come home on Wednesday.

Love,

Herb

June 13, 1942

Dear Mother, Dad, and Lou,

Received only one letter from you all week! What's the trouble?!

It was very hard to do any work around here because of the terrible heat. It was hot all day, and I don't think it has cooled down yet. How is the weather at home? If it's as hot as it is here, you better do some swimming. When I get home I expect to do quite a bit of swimming.

Since the regular session of summer school has started, we have been required to take physical education. So I have to buy a locker and equipment- $5! I play softball and tennis in my gym classes (after doing 25 pushups, other calisthenics, and ¼ mile run)! No fooling, they really make us work out. National defense– you know! Tomorrow the faculty is going to play a selected student body team of which I happen to be pitcher. However, I doubt if I'll pitch tomorrow.

As I told you before, we have our first test Monday. Therefore, I'm afraid I'll have to do some studying.

At present I'm listening to the A's lick the Indians. Did you go? If not, why not? If yes, how did you enjoy it?

Is the farm sold yet? How about some new places?

I haven't received that package from Phila. (the one you said Mom would send, Lewis) yet.

See you in three weeks.

Herb

September 30, 1942

Dear Mother and Dad,

I am rapidly getting settled once again.

As you can remember, before I left here this summer, I gave the janitor a $5 tip. Well, it pays dividends. During the summer he had my furniture in the room repainted, shampooed my rug and kept it nice and clean, and I'm the only fellow on the floor who got two brand-new blankets for my bed. If you would like, I will send home the quilt because I will have absolutely no use for it.

Tonight I went to see the movie "The Pied Piper." I would suggest that you see it if possible. It was a good enough picture, but there are parts in it that I disliked.

As yet I have not received my radio! Have you sent it yet? If not, please do so.

I think I told you my coat arrived and it looks darn nice.

There is one condition that I dislike very much this year. Bucknell has taken in twenty men from the Naval Air Corps to teach them the ground courses and flying. Well, the floor above us is like a big attic, and these 20 boys sleep there. Each morning they use our bathrooms and also at any other time of day. With these 20 fellows, it makes a total of <u>47</u> who use this bathroom. However, they must be out of the building by 7 a.m. so the bathroom will not be crowded in the morning. These fellows, during the summer, lived right here on the 4th floor, and again, thanks to the janitor, all rooms were taken except mine and another fellow's.

Have an 8 o'clock class every morning (except Sunday). Bet I don't cut any.

I gave out a $6 check today for a locker deposit in gym.

Am going to date this year if I have time.

Love,

Herb

November 11, 1942

Dear Mother and Dad,

Just came back from lab and received your letter.

The application for the air corps is identically the same as the one I filled out at home. Everything is going to be the same, except I will get into the Army Air Corps- Engineers "<u>Unassigned</u>." This <u>unassigned</u> means that I lack the necessary educational requirements to get into the Engineering division. Therefore, I will be in the reserves, but they will not be able to do anything at all to me until I complete my current school year which ends next June.

It is the custom, at present, to give all those in the reserves at least a six-month's notice to appear for service. This means if I get my call the day I become a senior, I will still graduate. Six months from June is January 1944, at which date I graduate. (We have to go to school all next summer, therefore if I pass everything this year, I'm as good as graduated). Of course, if we are invaded or really get in bad shape I will be called immediately. I think I have explained everything you asked for, but if you have any further questions, write and I will call you whenever you would like.

Enclosed you will find applications for the Naval Reserve. You are probably wondering why I am sending these also, but I think I would like to give the Navy a chance to get my services. Seriously though, the Navy comes up here next week, whereas the Air Corps won't be here for three weeks. Therefore, I believe in first come-first served. If I do get in the Navy, as long as I continue to remain in good standing here at BU, I am sure of graduating, since the Navy required a degree before taking Engineers.

For the Navy, I will need the following, which you can please obtain for me <u>immediately</u>:

a birth certificate

3 letters of recommendation

I have the three letters from before, but I will need three new ones for the Navy. I will use the others for the Air Corps, if I don't get in the Navy.

As for the birth certificate, I am enclosing the letter you sent me so that my name can be changed as soon as possible. It may have to be sent to Harrisburg, but tell them it's a rush job and maybe they will fix it up.

That about takes care of everything at present, except that I have to get my picture taken, which will cost some dough.

Also I spent $4.50 extra this week- I paid my dues for the A.S.M.E. [American Society of Mechanical Engineers]. Also as you probably noticed I am spending $12 a week instead of my expected $10. I eat about $10 worth of food.

What's going on down at Pitcairn's? Has the Navy taken over yet? Is the Major around? Write and let me know what's going on there! The last group of Navy men left Saturday and a new group comes in tomorrow. The old fellows were all talking about Pitcairn's.

Glad to hear you sold those two places!! Sell the next two and then worry about something else.

You know– it's funny– you have to work and worry to keep me here, and I have to work and worry to stay here.

Give Lewis my regards! Tell him to send me the prescription for the eyes as soon as possible.

See you–?

Love,

Herb

Please send all applications and letters back immediately! It is very important that I receive them before next Tuesday!

November 24, 1942

Typewritten letter

Dear Mother and Dad,

I am writing this letter today because I will probably be unable to write again until Thursday. I have a lot of reports to write, and I also have a big test on Wednesday.

There isn't much new up here except that the weather is getting very bad. We have had two snowfalls this year already, one was very light and the other was quite heavy.

By the way, we have admitted a new member into our graduate school across the hill. He is Mr. William fox, president of Fox Movitone News and Motion Picture Company. He was sent up here two weeks ago.

I may call home some night this week if I find it impossible to come home this weekend. However, fear not because our Christmas vacation begins in three weeks, and you better get used to being away from us while everything is going all right as far as we are concerned now. By that I mean within the next two years, at some time, you probably will not see me for perhaps a year, or even six months (which is a long time). To be truthful with you, if I ever get the time to think of home, I feel as if I must have forgotten to do something—that's how busy I am!!

So Mary got herself a fellow. I guess she wasn't just talking herself it into as you had thought.

I received the package this morning, and it was very good. The only trouble is that there was not enough of it.

How did you enjoy your stay with Lewis?

No other news now,

Love,

Herb

November 25, 1942

Typewritten letter

Dear Folks,

As I am writing this letter, I am writing a formal notice to Mr. Adolph Hitler, and Hirohito, telling them that their efforts have been wasted. Since the United States has begun drafting the youth of the nation, and among them is one Herbert Barness, the axis is doomed. I think you, as my parents, should know that I can really cause a lot of trouble as I have been doing for the 18 years and 359 days, or a total of 6929 days, which is 166,106 hours or 9,700,000 minutes.

Also as I am writing this letter, a thought comes into my mind how you used to yell at me in my childhood. When I was six, you called me a 12-year old; when I was 10, you called me 15; etc. Of course I realized I had the mentality of a person much older than myself, but to this day I cannot figure out why you tried to tell me I was much smarter than myself.

You also used to say "when will you grow up." You were mixed up someplace, but those days are gone forever because the days of my childhood are gone, the days of my boyhood are gone, and I may stand on a pedestal and shout, "Today I am a Man"!! I was always pretty much of a bother, but I can see it all now, and with all the arguments I had with both of you at last I will admit that I was frequently wrong, but since I inherited some of your stubbornness, I will say that I was also right part of the time.

If each minute of my life (not counting violin lessons) cost one-cent, to date I cost you $97,000 minus $400 per year deduction for income tax. Sort of expensive--don't you think?

I shall probably be unable to ever pay you back in dollars and cents, but that is not the true way of measuring the worth of something. Someday, somehow, someplace, when the world is normal again, your investment is going to start to pay dividends in more ways than one. This is a promise, and an answer to your question, "when will you grow up."

Tomorrow is Thanksgiving. Perhaps, because of the war many people will say there is nothing to be thankful for. The parents who lost their son or sons in battle will certainly say there is nothing to be thankful for, but somehow I have a different opinion of this idea. I am especially thankful this year because of things in general- nothing specific. I just like the outlook I have from this point.

If someone had asked me four years ago if I were going to college, I would have– and I did say– no. But here I am, one year to go to get my degree. I am not the smartest in the class, but I am not the dumbest. I am just about the average student, as far as marks go I am a little higher than the average Engineer.

One year to go! That is a very long time during war-time. If I don't get into the reserves very shortly, I will probably be drafted. To get into the reserves I must have a release from the draft board. Therefore, I will be home on Saturday afternoon and go see the draft board. Please call them up and find out if they are open on Saturday afternoon to answer questions. If they are not open, I will still be home, but I will have to send them a telegram. Do not ask them for a release because I don't need it until December 7.

See you Saturday,

Love,

Herb

December 15, 1942

Dear Mother and Dad,

As usual– I'm sorry I haven't written sooner, but– also as usual– I am very busy. Getting into the Army took lots of my man-hours, and with Christmas near, the profs want to keep us busy.

I had several tests last week, and this week it is absolutely awful! I had one test this morning, and I have three on Friday and two on Saturday.

Don't know whether you realized it or not, but I joined the Army exactly one year after the date of Pearl Harbor.

I really don't have much time, as it is getting very late, but I have a lot to write and if I can remember it all, you will have a long letter.

First of all, I am going to send home my laundry as I have done in previous years so that I won't have to carry so much. Also, if it is OK with you, I will send home my suitcase and come home the 24th with John Sigafoos (the boy from Doylestown). The reason I would like to do this is twofold. First of all, the train situation will be absolutely terrible, and secondly, I can do some work on the afternoon of the 23rd. I realize this doesn't give me much time at home before Christmas, but this isn't a normal year anyhow. Please let me know what you think, and I may call home if you so wish.

How are you making out in Phila.?

I will bring my wallet home.

When will Lewis be home?

Will see you soon,

Love,

Herb

CHAPTER 4

1943

ACTIVE DUTY

On March 8, 1943, Herb was called to active duty and appointed as Aviation Cadet, Meteorology Training. He went to Harrisburg, Pennsylvania and traveled to Washington, D.C., and then on to Boca Raton, Florida. He was assigned to Grand Rapids, Michigan in April, and then to Chanute Field in Illinois in September.

Herb received a commission as Second Lieutenant at the end of November. He was assigned to the Weather Squadron at New Castle Army Air Force Base in Wilmington, Delaware at the end of 1943.

March 8, 1943

Telegram to Herbert I Barness:

ORDERS RECEIVED FOR YOUR APPOINTMENT AND SHIPMENT AS PER METEOROLOGIST CADET FRIDAY MARCH 12TH STOP REPORT TO CADET BOARD HARRISBURG NINE THIRTY AM STOP ACHKNOWLEDGE RECEIPT IMMEDIATELY END.

March 8, 1943

Letter from the Aviation Cadet Examining Board, 4th and Market Streets, Harrisburg, PA

… the following named Air Force Enlisted Reservists are called to active duty and appointed Aviation Cadets (Ground Crew) Meteorology Training, effective March 12, 1943, and will proceed on that date from Harrisburg, Pennsylvania to the Air Force Technical School, Boca Raton, Florida, reporting upon arrival to the Commanding Officer thereat,

Barness, Herbert I. 13173461

The above named Aviation Cadets will be reimbursed for actual and necessary expenses which are incidental to this travel but not to exceed five ($5.00) dollars per day, per authority contained in Paragraph 7, AR 35-2580, dated June 29, 1942. The travel directed is necessary in the military service, and payment, when made, is chargeable to procurement authority FD 31 P 431-02 A 0425-23. The Transportation Corps will furnish the necessary transportation.

Train leaves Harrisburg at 1:50 p.m. on Friday, March 12, 1943.

Train arrives Washington DC at 5 p.m. and departs at 7:30 p.m.

Train arrives Boca Raton, Florida, on Saturday, March 13, 1943.

April 1, 1943

Stationery has a drawing of an airplane on it and says:

Army Air Forces Weather School, Grand Rapids, Michigan

Return address- Sqdn 7 40ᵗʰ Platoon

580ᵗʰ T.S.S.- A.A.F.

Room 339

Grand Rapids, Mich.

Dear Mother and Dad,

I sent a wire home tonite, which you probably have by now, and sent the slide rule.

Since I have already sent you my schedule, I need not tell you how tiring our day is. It keeps one so damn busy, we don't even have time to go to the bathroom– and I'm not kidding.

Everything is told to us, we just act on command. We have a time for each thing, and that's all we can do in the specified time.

The work isn't difficult– in fact no one seems to study at all. It isn't that we have no homework, we don't have enough time to do it so no one even starts.

Boy, do we keep our room clean! You ought to see it! You never saw anything so neat as our room.

Except for being so busy, there isn't anything else to it. The food is fine; the hotel, and rooms, are very nice. We have the best professors, and good classrooms.

We don't have much freedom, but I think I was meant to be a military man. A lot of the fellows are yelling about it, but I like it. It is rather easy and enjoyable. Whenever I march, or when we go to class, everything is so exact, it is very beautiful.

We should get at least one furlough before being sent overseas at the end of this course, but I don't know when that will be.

Love,
Herb

April 2, 1943

Dear Mom and Pop,

Boy, what a schedule! We get back at night and are so tired we can't do anything. The work is much easier than college, but the hours are terrible.

Other than the hours, this place is perfect. The food, living conditions, town, and everything else here is fine. I think this whole setup is going to be OK after I get used to it.

I don't think I ever mentioned it, but upon successful completion of this course, besides getting a commission, I will also get a Bachelor of Science degree in Meteorology.

Well, must study now.
Love,
Herb

P.S. You can send me some goodies.

April 8, 1943

Noon

Dear Folks,

There isn't much new around her today. Nice weather, regular classes, and just about nothing else.

Had a very good meal for lunch. Chops with sweet potatoes, orange flavored water, ice cream, etc. All the meals here are absolutely tops.

I don't recall if I ever explained the system of payment in the Army to you. We get paid 10 cents an hour for 24 hours a day, and anything over 24 hours a day we get time and one-half. This is more money than I ever made before though.

Speaking of money, this is what is going to happen to mine. We get paid $105 per month, out of which they take $30 immediately for food. My insurance policy for $10,000, made out to both of you, costs me $6.50 a month, or $75 - $6.50= $68.50. I subscribed to a $25 bond a month, which will be sent to you by the government, and which costs $18.75, or $68.50- $18.75= $49.25. I will be getting about $50 a month minus $3 a month for laundry, or $47. Out of this I would like to buy another bond for $18.75, or $46.75 - $18.75 equals $226 a month. Out of this I want to have enough money to go back to school, enough to buy mother a fur coat, enough to have a big 25th wedding anniversary party, and about 10 other things. Besides this, I will probably be spending 10 or 15 dollars a month here. Boy, I'm sure going to save my dough. There is one good thing about this, in 8 months the government is going to give me a raise to $183 per month base pay. This should help me balance my budget. Graduation day here is on or before November 27, so save your gas to drive out. November 27 will be 4 days before I will be 20.

That's about all.

Love,

Herb

P.S. Have you received my book yet? How about the tuition money from Bucknell? Please let me know about these two things.

April 8, 1943

8 p.m.

Dear Mother and Dad,

Received your letter with the clipping in it tonight. I can't figure out who put that write-up in the paper because I don't recall telling you what courses I am taking. Did you put it in? Do you know who put it in? If you do, please let me know since I am very curious. If you don't know, can you find out?

Received a letter from Selma this evening. She told me that Uncle Hyman and she were going to visit Marvin, by plane. Maybe you and Mother ought to fly out here. Perhaps when I graduate you and Mom and Lewis can get here. I would like you to see us march around singing songs and doing all sort of stuff that is as accurate as a machine. The songs we sing are cheerful songs, not like "what the hell are we marching for." The men that are here are of a high enough caliber to take things the right way.

Well, that's about all.

Love,
Herb

Have my books or school money arrived?

April 13, 1943

Dear Mother and Dad,

When you receive this letter, you probably won't be in Phila. working, due to rain. It either rained on Tuesday or Wednesday (13th or 14th) at home. At least that's what I predict. There are rain clouds headed your way, but they may miss you. I don't know that much about meteorology yet. However, from looking at several of the charts, I can tell you what kind of weather you are going to have for the next ten days. These aren't my predictions, but those of the experienced men here. If I did mention the weather, and if anyone ever heard of it, I would be court-martialed as a spy. We have gotten written orders here that we read, and as soon as we finish reading them, we must burn the papers.

I don't think I ever mentioned it, but one of the best teachers here is a Jew. He was head of the Meteorology department at MIT before the Army called him. He is a Captain, and since we can't talk to Captains, I do not know him at all. Even if we could talk, I probably wouldn't know him.

We have had quite a few tests here so far, and I have made out very well in them. I hope I can keep it up, but I am not going to study until absolutely necessary.

Myself, and two of my roommates, went for a walk out in the country yesterday, and some Doctor came along in a beautiful car and took us all around. That's the way most of the people feel towards the cadets out here. Very very friendly.

It will be practically impossible for me to write every day, because I am writing to at least 25 people. It's a full time job.

Love,
Herb

April 15, 1943

Dear Mother and Dad,

Just came back from getting my second typhoid shot, second tetanus shot and vaccination. Boy, they shoot us full of that stuff. Tetanus and vaccination in the left arm, and typhoid in the right arm.

I don't think I ever mentioned it, but I got my first typhoid and first tetanus at Boca Raton. We must have three of each, so next week I will probably get my last two shots.

You know how I just love to take shots! However, I'll admit I hated like hell to get them, but I never felt anything. It was all over in about 5 seconds. There are supposed to be some reactions after a few hours, though.

Glad you finally got the OK to build, but am wondering how you are going to do it. It will certainly build up Warrington though. Probably by the time I come home in June, you will already be building there. However, if you are short 5 or 6 men, I am afraid I will not be able to help you, since we aren't allowed out of uniform.

I will have my picture taken as soon as the government decides to give us our cadet issue. This may not be for several weeks though. Maybe in two or three weeks.

Things in school are just about the same. Long hours- easy work. I have been off the post every night, and on Saturday night and Sunday. Perhaps I will start studying next month.

That's about all,

Love,

Herb

April 18, 1943

Dear Mother and Dad,

Today marks the 5th full week of Army life for me. In these five weeks I have learned many things. I have learned how to march with men, stand at attention, clean my room daily, polish my shoes and keep my uniforms in perfect condition daily, and I have learned how to take and give orders.

Six weeks ago in this time, I never actually thought I would be in the Army so soon. I was hoping I would get my call, but it seemed as though they didn't want me. When I would call home on Sunday morning (about 2 p.m.), you would say: "I'm afraid you are going to be disappointed, you will be able to finish school." But you knew that was only wishful thinking, and I knew damned well I was wishing you were wrong.

If you can remember, since November 1941, even before the United States was in the war, I was trying to get in the Air Force. At that time, however, it was the Canadian Air Force.

On February 16, 1942, I was supposed to report to New York to take a transport plane for Canada. But we were already in the war at this time, so I thought I might as well try to get in our Air Forces.

On February 26, I went to take my physical for the Naval Air Corps– but was rejected before I even started, for at that time I was 18 years old, and the age limit was from 20 to 27.

From here on, you know the rest of the story. It was a try at West Point, at the Navy, at the Army Air Corps, again at the Navy, and once again at the Army Air Forces, but no luck. Finally, I got into the Enlisted Reserve Corps, and then the place I was waiting for for 19 years.

And here I am– a soldier– a weatherman– a student. This is my life, and it is a damn good life. I always said college was no place for any man during war, and the more I get into the way of life around here, the more I wish I had been in the Army since November, 1941.

Many people complain about the Army, but these people will complain about anything that they do. The Army does not have a picnic for us every day, yet neither does any other organization. We work, we have a routine we must follow, we know what must be done– and it's up to us to do it. Thus far, the type of work is the same as college, but it is much more interesting, and we have more free time. Since I have been here, I have only stayed in 2 nights, out of a total of 21 days (and nights).

Of course, there are a great number of inefficiencies in the Army– that is why the enlisted personnel does not like it. However, the Army is like a big company running with 11 million men, and you know what the efficiency is of a company running with 50 men.

I don't know if you understand the term "enlisted men," but I am not an "enlisted man." An enlisted man is a private, corporal, or sergeant. We are cadets, and are addressed as "cadet" or "mister." Enlisted men are addressed as "hey you." Our rating is above a master sergeant, and below a second Lieutenant. This may be one reason why a cadet never complains about anything– even in private.

Being a weather-man probably sounds funny to you, and when people ask you what I am doing, you may have a hard time explaining it. I can tell you what my job shall be, but if you really want to know what a meteorologist does, just ask a pilot or bombardier sometime– they know what our job is.

The pilot and bombardier, navigator, and anyone who flies, knows what a meteorologist is. They can tell you because they know that the weatherman holds their life in his hands. It is all team work; the weatherman and mechanic sees that the pilot and bombardier get in the air safely, and come down safely.

A commanding officer may order his whole pursuit squadron into the air, but if the meteorologist says "no," the men don't fly. Our motto is "Sustineo Alas"– Latin meaning "I Sustain the Wings." Yes, some day I shall keep those planes flying– and keep those wings up high.

Someone may also say to you that I shall have a pretty soft time of the Army after I get my commission. In fact, that is what I thought myself. I still think this, because I can get along as well as the next fellow, but there is more to it than that.

Although all our work here is strictly confidential now, I can tell you something that has been driven into us since the first day we came here. In fact, the colonel gave us a talk the first Sunday morning, and told us to expect to leave the country as soon as we are commissioned. I didn't want to tell you this because I know how you will feel, but you will hear about it sooner or later. Graduation is around November 27, and unless the war changes one helluva lot, I should be in Europe for Christmas. And it's plenty OK with me.

I have been exchanging letters with Marvin, and it seems as thought the cadet system there is exactly the same here, except of course, we go to school, whereas he flies.

Remember– Nothing can stop the Army Air Corps– except the weather.

Love,

Herb

P.S. Received a letter from Eli today.

May 23, 1943

Dear Lou,

If you still have my pictures, you may take note of the uniform I have on, again. With the exception of the insignia, you too shall soon be wearing the same type uniform.

The hat, insignia, patches (insignia on the arm), and low-cut shoes are part of the cadet issue I am wearing. As for the blouse, shirt, pants, socks, tie, and underwear (don't think you can see that here), they are identical as to the type you get.

Enclosed is a "patch." As you can see this is not the regular Air Corps insignia, but rather the well-known "cadet insignia." These patches are worn 4" from the bottom of the right sleeve on all shirts, coats (except raincoats), and jackets. (The tailor charges 12 cents to sew them on).

The brass insignia that you wear will not be the same type as you used to wear home. You were wearing the pin-type, which only officers and cadets may wear. You will soon wear a round brass button with the pedusa (?) [he meant caduceus] on one lapel and a round brass button with a US on the other lapel. I think you can see the type US and wings I am wearing.

I'll be able to tell you all about some of the other stuff you may want to know when I see you at home. If, however, you have any questions that you want to know immediately, let me know and I'll call you on the 30th.

As I said before, if you know definitely that you go into uniform as soon as you return to school, get rid of all unnecessary clothing and papers. You will have a job keeping your room clean as is without having any unnecessary papers laying around. It is rather doubtful if you will be allowed to have any magazines in your room also. We can't keep any magazines, papers, or eat any sort of food in our rooms.

Your military life will not be nearly as rigid as mine, since I am getting actual cadet training, and you will only be an enlisted man. We have to take a lot of "chicken shit," but the enlisted men have to take the big shit. That is, they nail us for any little thing, whereas they will let you get away with a lot.

This "chicken shit" is what Marvin [cousin] is always bitching about, and it's what makes this life more interesting. I like it because it keeps us on our toes and gives us a feeling of equality. Marv dislikes it because he never had to get up at 6 a.m. and have a prescribed day. You will find it absolutely the same as your present status, except you, as an individual, will probably like it better.

In college, as you can remember, my spirits used to go up and down. I was ready to quit on numerous occasions, and I was flunking twice as many times. It's different here; the work is tough– in fact it is now tougher than anything I ever had, but our morale is exceptionally high. Everybody screws around, loafs, gold-bricks [shirks or slacks], and has a good time. We know about 10% will wash out before the first 11 weeks are over, so we do as little work as possible and yet keep going. Of course, some of the boys are pretty damn good. At present, I study two solid hours a night, which happens to be a "cadet order." After mid-term, the Colonel in charge of the Academic section gave the order that no one may go to bed before 11 p.m., and quiet hours must be maintained between 9 and 11. In college, we would bitch if we were ordered to do this. Here, no one says a damn thing, and all orders are always carried out in the Army. If I wanted to write a letter between 9 and 11 some night, I couldn't do it. If I tried and got caught, I would be walking penalty tours.

When I see you I shall tell you as much as I can.

Until then,

Herb

June 28, 1943

Dear Lou,

You're in the Army now chump! How do you like your new summer outfit?

Haven't found out anything about my grades because the Army doesn't give out marks. It's either pass or flunk.

It's so god damn hot out here that our sweat evaporates, rises, condenses, and we get thunderstorms.

If you see Beigel (?) tell him I offer him my sympathy. It's a shame he got in the Navy.

Last night we went out to an amusement part in G.R. [Grand Rapids]. I was thinking of you as we banged into each other in the scooter cards. Remember that stuff in Wildwood?

Do you know your General Orders? Have you received your outfit yet? What kind of shoes? Do you have your dog tags? How many "short-arms" have you had?

Send me all the dope– dope.

A/C Barness

July 1, 1943

Dear Lou,

I am not being entertained in "Climatology" by some dull lecturer from Harvard. I really don't know where he is from, but I can't imagine anyone being so dry coming from any other school but Harvard.

Well boy, how in the hell do you like the Army? How many hours a day do you drill? Do you continue drilling after this first week? If so, how often?

What type uniform have you received? Did you get two pairs of high GI's? Have they started giving you shots? How is the food? How many fellows in your room? Why the change in room? Are the Navy fellows in uniform? When do you get a furlough?

I have written to Sonny, so I suppose I'll hear from him soon. Still haven't heard from Marvin, but Harriet wrote and said he expects to be shipped to Arkansas. He should be getting his wings soon.

I haven't heard whether I passed or washed out yet, but I shall probably hear very soon. I've got my fingers crossed, but I think they will let me stick.

Can't think of anything else,

A/C Barness, H.I.

July 5, 1943

Dear Pvt,

What the hell is the trouble man! Long time no hear!

See here, <u>Pvt</u>. Barness. Boy that's great stuff– you go to school for 'steen years, and all they make you is a pvt. That's about all the good a quack is, I guess.

Went to seen an air show yesterday, and it was quite nice. Saw them fly those big CG-4A gliders around. Hope to see a few ball games in Detroit sometime soon.

Am still expecting to be called in by the Colonel about getting washed out, so keep your fingers crossed. I have been doing much better this semester than I did last, however.

Herb

July 10, 1943

Dear Lou,

Sorry I haven't written sooner, but I thought I would be changing my address this week. The old washing machine is working double time these days, so I will soon be a pvt. too– unless they decide they need good men with low grades. When they see the grades I have been getting this semester though, they may change their minds. I have been on the ball– or quasi (that's a good word), so this term I have even surprised myself.

Bill Bloom was in town yesterday. As you probably remember, he said he expected to be here sometime. Well, I got to see him during my free hour last night. I took him thru the post, gave him some GI Beer, showed him the classrooms, etc.; then we went out and had a few drinks, and the hour was up. It sure was good to see him.

Want to get this letter off now, so will sign off,
A/C B.

July 27, 1943

Dear Lou,

In case I forget, HAPPY BIRTHDAY! You are getting in the marrying age boy– start looking!!!! [Lew is 22.]

Last week I was room orderly–yesterday I walked 3 tours. Then, to top it off, I was a guard from 8 to 9 last night. I am quite glad I walked those tours, it can be chalked up as some more experience.

I believe you can realize how important the weather man is, after reading that clipping you sent me. Last week, the chemical warfare branch of the Army, and Army Air Corps (each has its own chem warfare) asked for volunteers from this school to help in the gas warfare. That is, after the fellows graduate, they will be put in chem war. I want to keep as far away from gas as possible, so I didn't sign up.

I don't know when we will be getting off– or even if we do get off. However, should we get a furlough, it will be in six weeks. Will probably be able to let you know in about 2 weeks.

That's all,
Herb

P.S. What is ASTU-SCSA?

August 26, 1943

A post card to his parents that has a picture of an aviator with the words "So we'll meet again. Buy More War Bonds"

Will be in Phila.- 7 a.m. Sunday, September 5. School over noon on Saturday. Am coming home via Detroit.

Love,
Herb

September 1, 1943

Dear Folks,

Yesterday we had gas mask drill, and pistol and machine-gun practice.

First we went into a gas chamber with our gas masks on, then they sprayed in some tear gas, and we had to take our masks off. That is really awful. Your skin burns, your eyes tear, and one feels miserable.

After we got over that, we went out to the pistol range. There we shot 50 rounds with a pistol, and 25 rounds with a machine-gun. I can see now why men get shell-shocked. My ears are still ringing.

Received an announcement of Marv's graduation yesterday. He graduated on Monday, so it was too late to write or telegraph and congratulate him. I figured he probably left for his furlough– if he got one.

See you Sunday,

Love,

Herb

September 13, 1943

Stationery from Army Air Forces Chanute Field Illinois

Return address on envelope: A/C Barness

Flight F, Plat. 2

35th T.S.S.

Chanute Field, Ill.

Dear Folks,

Tried to call yesterday, but couldn't get a line thru.

This is one helluva big place, about 35,000 men. We live in Bays here, and of course we got the best of them all. They call our quarters Buckingham Palace- but I liked the hotel better.

Amongst other things, this is a 4 engine flying school, mechanics school, weather school, engineer school, propeller school, and millions of others. Before the 11 weeks is up, I hope to see the whole place.

So far, I have seen 2 theatres and about a dozen stores here. So you see it is really a big place. Don't know where to mail this yet, but will soon find out.

Love,

Herb

September 14, 1943

Return address:

A/C Barness

Bay C- 304

35th T.S.S.

Chanute Field, Ill.

Dear Folks,

I have exactly 15 minutes a day to write letters here, and this time is from 6:30 a.m. to 6:45 a.m.

They are keeping us hundreds of times busier here than at Grand Rapids. We are up at 6; reveille 6:30; breakfast formation 6:45; drill formation 7:30; drill 7:30-10:00; school from 10:00 – 1:00 p.m.;

lunch 1:00- 2:00; school 2:00 straight thru to 7 p.m.; supper 7:00 p.m.; formation 7:45 p.m.; supervised study from 8 to 10 p.m. Lights out at 10:30 p.m.

It's the stiffest pace I have ever had. In fact, it is getting me down already. That is, I would like to have a little free time during the day, and I think they will soon realize that we need some break. However, it isn't going to be very difficult to keep this up for 11 weeks.

Received a letter from Viv, by way of Grand Rapids.

Packages are always welcome around here.

Will try to call on Sunday, if I can get to a telephone booth before a million others.

Love,

Herb

P.S. Correct address on envelope.

September 14, 1943

Dear Lou,

Boy, I wish to hell I was back in GR. It was a lot better up there.

Our rooms down here are very nice. We live in "Bays," with about 60 men to a bay, in a very very large brick building. Our barracks are definitely the best on the post since we have the only officer candidate here. Our barracks are called "Buckingham Palace."

We have an enormous mess hall, and if anything, the food here is better than that of GR. The service is quick, efficient, and very good meals. We have a menu posted for each meal, and always have a big choice. This is straight stuff– no shit!

They have about 50 or 60 2nd Looey pilots here going to 4-engine school. The type of plane here is the B-17 "Flying Fortress." Saturday afternoon we went thru 4 of these jobs while they were being serviced for take-offs. They are really neat– but bigger than hell. Other planes here are the P-40, P-39, P-36, P-51, Lockheed Hudsons, trainers, B-26, and about 10 other models (including B-24's).

Will finish this letter as soon as I get back– and I'll tell you why I'd rather be in GR.

Just came back from drill, and have about 10 minutes until class formation. Here is/are the disadvantages of Chanute:

First call: 06:00

Reveille (formation outside): 06:30

Breakfast (formation outside): 06:45

Drill and PT formation (outside: 07:30- 10:30

Formation for class: 10:30

Lunch: 13:00

Class: <u>14:00</u> – <u>19:00</u>

Supper: 19:00

Formation for <u>supervised</u> study: <u>2000-2200</u>

Lights out at 22:30. So you see we are busier than shit!!!! The only time I'll have for letters is between 6:30 and 6:45 and here and there during a 10-minute break. I just hope I last.

This is a beautiful field, and I only hope to spend some time on the flying line.

Oh yes- there are approximately 1000 WAACS [Women's Army Auxiliary Corps] stationed here. They are the only ones (besides the officers) who are allowed to eat in our mess hall. Some, but very few, are nice.

Chanute Field is on the border of Rantoul, Ill; and about 20 miles from Champaign, home of the University of Illinois. Also about 150 miles south of Chicago.

The field has about 35,000 men, most of whom are going to different types of TTS schools.

That's about all for now– and a few weeks.

Herb

September 15, 1943

Dear Folks,

Nothing new around here, except things are settling down in general.

I wrote to Lewis yesterday, but I doubt very much if I shall be able to correspond with anyone else. This schedule is really terrific. They have, however, given us ½ hour free in the morning, and ½ hour between 10 and 10:30 at night. Lights go out at 10:30.

The food here is about the same as Grand Rapids. We have a special mess hall which only we cadets and the WAACS may use.

I don't know if I mentioned it, but there are about 60 of us living in this room, but the room was built to accommodate 150, so we are not at all crowded.

If you don't mind, will you please see if you can get hold of a small portable radio. There isn't much chance, so far as we know, to leave the post on weekends, so it would sort of cheer things up.

That's about all.

Love,

Herb

P.S. As I said before– will try to call on Sunday if I can.

September 16, 1943

Instead of a stamp on this envelope, Herb wrote the words FREE

Dear Folks,

Working harder than usual, but am slowly getting used to this race. We never have time to walk anyplace– it's always run or be late.

Yesterday they had a brand new B-24 bomber here– the kind Marvin is learning to fly. They seem to be about the best bomber we have.

If you have Marvin's address, please sent it, so if I get the chance I can write.

Love,

Herb

September 19, 1943

Dear Doc [I am assuming that Lewis is in medical school at Harvard now, or at least he wants/knows that's where he is going next!],

What the hell's the trouble man!!! I send you one letter and <u>20</u> postcards in one week, and what do I get– nothing.

Before I forget- looking around the post the other day, I went in the hospital here–which is damn near as big as your "Bent-Peter," [I am assuming that this is a reference to Peter Bent Brigham Hospital in Boston] and quite nice. When I went on the second floor, just as I stepped off the elevator, I saw a guy running down the hall clinging on to his clothes and running faster than hell. Right behind him was a pretty nurse carrying a tea-kettle full of steaming-hot water– also running faster than hell trying to catch the guy. Then directly behind the nurse was a Doctor, running after the nurse who was running after the soldier. The Doctor kept yelling to the nurse: "No-No-Nurse– you misunderstood me, I said, "Prick his Boil"– "Prick his boil." Amen!!

This work is really getting me down, but next Sunday I am going up in a B-1. I have a parachute reserved and everything, so here's hoping.

WRITE.

Herb

September 20, 1943

Dear Folks,

Sorry I couldn't speak to both of you yesterday, but I had been trying to call all day until I got you.

I went out on the flying line yesterday, and next Sunday I expect and hope to go up in a [B-17] Flying Fortress. I could have gone up yesterday, but I got out there too late. They fly around for 3 hours at a time.

If you get a chance, will you please see if you can get me a small portable radio. I don't want a very large radio, in fact I want a small one– the kind that is carried on a strap over the shoulder. If you can't find any like that, any good portable will do– but not too big.

That's all,

Love,

Herb

September 23, 1943

Dear Lou,

The time here at Chanute, although fully occupied, is going slower than hell. This may be due to various reasons, but the biggest reason is they have cut our maximum sleeping time to 7 ½ hours, and we now have 10 hours of classes, 2 hours of PT, 3 hours for meals, and we must study for 1½ hours. If you think this time is figured out too exact, you ought to be here. Everything is done like clockwork.

Our commanding officer is a Brigadier General, and he seems like a pretty good boy.

If I get my commish, I shall be damn happy, for at present, that bar looks very very far off. Next week we start getting measured for uniforms and stuff.

Herb

September 26, 1943

Dear Lou,

What's good for a cold? And don't tell me sleep and lots of rest goddammit. I can't get either.

This letter is going to be written rather hastily, as I would like to get some sleep (1 hour) before we go to class at 8 o'clock tonight. I have a bitchy headache.

Couldn't go up today because too many went up last Sunday, and as usual, they put a restriction on going up.

No other news,

Herb

September 30, 1943

Addressed to P.F.P. L.A. Barness

442 Vanderbilt Hall

Boston, Mass.

Dear Lou,

Eight more weeks and 2 more days to go– if I last– and I am plenty worried about staying. They are giving us the works in these last weeks to see if we can keep up with them. Just to give you an example of what we do: Last semester we would complete a map and analysis (which includes 3 minor maps and forecasts) in 15 hours. Last week we did the same thing in 3 hours. This week we do 2 maps and analyses in 3 hours, which is practically impossible– but must be done.

We do practice flight forecasts for bombers and pursuit jobs daily, plus spot forecasts for 12, 24, and 36 hours. A spot forecast is a forecast for 1 individual station.

How are you making out? When will you get a furlough?

Received a letter from Beardsleys. They have the route all picked out to come up here.

That's all,

Herb

October 5, 1943

Dear Folks,

Well, we are well on our way in the 4th week here. The new class started yesterday, but we have absolutely nothing to do with them. Our schedules are different, and the only time we are together is for breakfast.

There are no "companies" in the Air Corps. We have Squadrons and Flights.

Joe Louis [famous boxer known as the Brown Bomber] is coming here tomorrow night to put on an exhibition, but we will be in class.

That's all,

Love,

Herb

October 7, 1943

Dear Folks,

In case you don't know it, aside from Saturdays and Sundays, yesterday was the first day I didn't write since I have been here. We had 1 hour off yesterday morning, so immediately after reveille I went to sleep for an hour.

There isn't anything new around here. We are, so far, having beautiful weather.

Don't know if I ever told you, but every Friday from 8 a.m. to 5 p.m. we must wear gas masks. That is, we must carry them, and sometimes a raid signal is given and we put them on.

Lewis wrote and said his vacation was from December 18-28. If I do graduate, it will be on Nov. 27, so I guess I won't see Lewis unless we get a furlough.

Love,

Herb

October 11, 1943

Dear Lou,

Jesus H. man! What the hell seems to be the trouble– me no receive letters from sad honorable doctor for long time.

By the way chum, did you ever receive a 20 greenback from Cadet B?? I sent one for part payment of anniversary gift, and sure would like to know if you received it. Please let me have the dope immediately.

Boy, I really have a lot to tell you now, but it will take too long to write, so I'll do it briefly. First of all, saw Joe Louis vs. George Nicholson, and Ray Robinson vs. Jack Wilson, last Thursday night. Sat in the third row from the ring, so can tell you all about the boys. They just put on an exhibition. (Jack Wilson was former Welterweight champ– Robinson present champ).

Secondly (and this is good), Saturday night six of us guys went to the next town, rented a hotel room, and pissed to the gills. We each bought a pint, left it in the room, and then went out and started putting served stuff away. As it ended up we got picked up by an MP and SP, thrown out of 2 hotels and a taxi, and finally 2 of the guys went out in the park to sleep with a few women. It was really some weekend.

At all times I was sober enough to know what I was doing, and I told one of our Captains (instructor) that he better go home before two many gadgets come in the bar, or else he will get tossed out. He told me to go to hell (he was drunker than I) and he was up in our room with us for awhile. I'll never do that again (until next week).

Well chum, let me hear from you sometime in the near future. I may have a change of address as soon as they start the washing machine again.

Lots of luck,
Herb

November 1, 1943

Dear Lou,

I am writing this note from surface charts class– and if I get caught, I'm a dead duck!

Surface charts is the most important course we are taking– in fact, it sums up all the theory and practical work into one. I finished my maps, so I have a little time to waste.

Wednesday we filled in preference forms for classification when commissioned. The main points were: 6 choices of type of work interested in (i.e., what kind of weather job); 6 choices of area interested in working.

Here are my choices:
1. Tactical (assigned as squadron weather officer)
2. Weather Reconnaissance (fly– and get flt. pay)
3. Ground forces
4. Base station
5. Instructor
6. Research

Areas I would like to go to, are:

1. Mediterranean
2. Alaska
3. China
4. South Pacific
5. India
6. Hawaii

We were interviewed today, and after a short discussion, I was recommended for weather reconnaissance. This is really my best bet, and if I can do anything to get it, I'm really going to try.

Oh yes, in our applications, there was a space for remarks, and I wrote; "I am extremely interested in being sent to an immediate combat zone as a reco officer. If my vision were 20/20, I would have been a pilot."

This doesn't mean too much, because the customary thing for new graduates is to send them to a base station for training. (A base station is any large field in the US).

Very, very sorry to hear that you were rejected from PGH [assuming this was Philadelphia General Hospital, but I am not positive] but guess you'll just have to be satisfied with Pennsy. You better pick one in Phila.– even if it must be Penn– for I know damned well I won't be around very long.

About washing out– I still may go, but my hopes are very high the way I have been hitting the exams recently.

I already have all uniforms, and they really run up into the dough. Paid $44.50 for blouse and pants; $9 for shirts; $12 for pinks; $55 Trench Coat (not required); $30 short coat; $10 rain coat; $15 hat, etc. I think it will cost me about $300 by the time I'm all set.

Well, son, keep your fingers crossed for me, and I'll hope to hell you get into a hospital soon. You know what you're doing, but suggest you get Bellet to help you in PGH. Get on the ball and get set!

Good luck,
Herb

November 3, 1943

Dear Folks,

Am still exceptionally busy, but ever since I have been warned to get to work, I haven't gotten a grade under 90. If I started this 8 months ago, I wouldn't be worrying now for I'd easily be in the top 10%. However, I'm not sorry about it– as long as I don't wash out, because I had a good time and did a minimum of work.

If I have time now, this is going to be a long letter.

First of all, I would like you to get my sunglasses fixed that I left home. I suppose you know where they are, and I would like to have them when and if I graduate, because it is a current policy to ship the officers overseas as soon as possible. If I graduate, I'll probably be out of the US by Christmas. As you know, this won't make me the least bit angry.

As for the glasses, I suggest you take them in immediately, since it may take some time to get them fixed.

Secondly, as you know, I have already gotten my uniform. I only bought the required clothing, but I did get almost the best I could. However, most of the stuff was regular requirements, but I spent a good deal of money. We were paid on Sunday, and I paid $40 on uniforms, out of my $46 pay. I do not need any money now, and I won't need any until I am (if I am) commissioned. At this time, I expect to need some cash to carry me thru my first month as an officer, since we don't get paid in advance in the Army. As an officer though, we must pay for our room and board in advance, then at the end of the month, the government comes thru as usual. Therefore, until I get my first pay, if possible, I would like to borrow $100-$150 so that I can meet all expenses. As I said, I won't need this until you come up here for graduation- if I graduate.

As yet I haven't written to Beardsleys, so if you write to them soon, tell them I shall write as soon as I find out anything definite.

This letter was started last night– didn't have time to finish, so here goes today.

This morning we signed discharge papers. It is customary to be discharged from the Army 24 hours before receiving a commission, and since papers must go to Washington, we started signing today.

If I do graduate, I think I am going to need some winter clothing, since I will be sent, as I have it figured out, to a nice cold climate.

No other news now, keep your fingers crossed for the next 3 weeks.

Love,

Herb

November 5, 1943

Dear Folks,

Perhaps you have been wondering why I stopped writing daily, so I'll tell you. As you know, I used to write every morning immediately after Reveille, which was at 6:30. Well, as soon as we were allowed, immediately after Reveille, I used to go back to sleep until 8 o'clock formation. However, I think we have to stay up now, so my letters may continue.

I suggest you make plans for being here the 29th of November— the day of graduation. This is on a Monday, so I guess you will have to take off from about Saturday to Tuesday or Wednesday— my birthday. I'm still not sure I will graduate, so I wouldn't say much about it, but I think it would be a good idea to get reservations to get here.

Again I started this letter yesterday and will finish today, Friday.

Glad to hear people are starting to move in on Barness Road. Hope you'll have them all finished soon.

Will speak to you Sunday, so won't write any more.

Love,

Herb

November 5, 1943

Dear Lou,

Well, three weeks to go, and I still don't know what the hell the score is. The only thing I can do now is hope they don't get me. The latest rumors around here have it that the next, and last, washout will be next week– so keep your fingers crossed.

By the way, we have just been advised that Metro's have an excellent opportunity for flying training– if they can pass the physical. Therefore, once again, for the n-th time, what the hell can I do for my eyes. I have about 4 weeks to work on them (if I get said commission), so give me the lowdown on any exercises (eye), pills, drops, etc., that can help me. There's nothing I'd like more than to become a pilot. My latest physical, about 4 weeks ago (physical for commission), I read 20/50. The requirement for flying is only 20/30 now, so with a little work, I think I could do the trick. If I could get in, then I'd get contact lenses and fly with them. Give me the dope— doc!!

Well chum, that's about all for now, will let you know of any new action as soon as I hear any.

Best of luck,
Herb

November 9, 1943

Dear Lou,

Am sitting here now waiting for a lecture in "Long Range Forecasting" to begin. A long-range forecast is any forecast that is over 48 hours.

As you can see, I'm still here at Chanute, and I haven't been washed yet. This has pulled up my spirits for the time being, since we only have a short time to go. However, they may pull a washout anytime this week, or the early part of next week.

The folks intended to come up here for graduation, but I'm afraid I'll have to stop that plan. A notice was put up yesterday stating, "No accommodations can be made for guests at the graduation exercises, but a 10 day leave shall be granted to each graduate."

This sounds pretty good to me; now all I have to do is graduate– which may be quite a job yet.

I haven't written to Beardsleys for a long time, but I'll have to write to them tonite, so they may write home and find out what the folks expect to do.

Glad to hear you got in PGH, but I really didn't doubt that you would get in.

By the way, I may be sent to Yale for 5 months for Engineering (AAF) if I so desire (if I graduate!) I don't think I'll take it though, because I've wasted enough time in school for the duration. However, if I could get into flying– here I come.

That's about all,

Best of luck,

Herb

November 9, 1943

Dear Lou,

Received your letter several minutes ago, and am taking precious moments out of my 2 study hours to write you (I don't do anything in these 2 hours anyhow).

As you know, I used to take those damn "A" pills daily. They helped somewhat, but I believe a diet of special foods would also help. Of course, this is only a layman's opinion. I shall take your advice and try to get as much rest as possible.

One of the fellows in our bay came down with scarlet fever yesterday, so about 30 of us are getting examined daily. The Doc (a Major) looks at our throats and stomachs each morning. This just started this morning and shall end on the 15th. Better not mention it to the folks since Mom will start worrying.

I don't think I'll try to get into Engineering, but if I have the educational qualifications I will give Intelligence a try. My thoughts are rambling all over the goddamn place because I want to get the hell out of here and get overseas, while the folks keep begging me to get into another Tech School. After going to school this long, I feel I am ready to do some work, and the experience I shall get will be excellent.

I still may wash out, but as you can probably tell, my hopes have brightened.

If I do graduate, I'll come up and see you the following weekend, since we could probably raise more hell there than at home.

I already wrote home and told them what I want for my birthday.

Best of luck,

Herb

P.S. Received a first-day issue [This is a postage stamp on a stamped envelope on the first day the issue is authorized for use.]

November 13, 1943

Dear Folks,

Just received a letter from Beardsleys, but they haven't received my last letter yet.

I also received your letter this morning with $10. Although I don't need any money now, you know I can always use it. Besides, I want you to know that the thought behind the money was worth more than the money itself.

When one has been away from home for a long time (this is my 3rd year- including college), it's the little things that mean more than the big ones. As you well know, I'm not much of the sentimental type, but rather I have always been sort of a rough and ready guy. Therefore, there is always very little I like to say except "thank you." However, every time I have ever asked for anything since I have been in the Army, you have always come through immediately. Do not think I am feeling so humble because of the $10, but rather it is an accumulation of a package here, money there, a package, etc. As far as I know, I have never been refused anything during my stay here in the Army. Someday I hope to be able to repay for you many things.

At present, I have absolutely no intentions of entering another school. I feel I have been hanging around here for a long enough time.

I will try to call Sunday and have you send me a foot-locker via Railway Express.

Saw in the Intelligencer that you and Beggs are in charge of the next Lions [Club- a "secular, non-political service organization"] meeting.

That's all,

Love,

Herb

November 17, 1943

Dear Lou,

Again I am writing to you from class– only this time I am listening to a dry lecture on Oceanography. It isn't a bad course, but there just isn't much interesting stuff. Of course, I felt the same way about Climatology for the first few weeks.

I am not completely completed with the purchasing of my outfit. I expect to go over to the clothier and get everything tomorrow. Now all I have to do is graduate, which at this time, I expect to do. Boy, I'm really going to look sharp in that zoot-soot.

Do you expect to get home sometime between the 1st and the 10th, or would you want me to come up and see you? I called home last Sunday and was told you were going to try to make it home. The folks said they haven't seen you for 3 months– which is impossible because you were home when I was.

Boy, they are really treating us great around here now. We F.O. all the time (except in class), and no one seems to care. The spirit is, of course, very high, and everyone is all set to go.

I am getting my birthday presents a little early this year due to the circumstances. Mom is sending me a foot-locker, and a pair of gloves. Those 2 things complete my ensemble!

This morning we signed our final physical reports, and filled out our form #66. You too shall do that some day. (Form 66 is a personal history form– which you fill out in the Army about 'steen times). We signed those forms– Herbert I. Barness, 2nd Lt., AC. First time I had every signed anything like that.

That's about all,

Best of luck,

Herb.

November 17, 1943

Dear Folks,

Each day means a day closer to graduation, which doesn't make me the least bit sad. For the past 5 weeks I have been on the ball, so the way it looks now, I have a good chance of graduating. We get some sort of degree in Meteorology at graduation.

I read in the Intelligencer that the Lions were having their annual on December 7. There are a few things I would like to say about this. As you know we got into the war on December 7, 1941. Also as you know, I joined the Army on December 7, 1942. Thirdly, this year on or about December 7 of this year, I will be on my way out to my post. More than likely it will be the US for a while, but then I'll be on my way to see action. Since I will be leaving on the 6th or 7th, I suggest you make reservations for yourself at the Lions party.

You see, my ten-day leave (if I graduate) will start on the 29th and therefore end on the 8th. This means I'll have to be on my new post on the 8th, and should I be sent to California, or down South, it will take quite a slice out of my leave. (An officer doesn't get a furlough; they call it a "leave.")

We are supposed to buy our train tickets this weekend, so whenever you can spare it, I would appreciate it if you could send me a little dough. I don't know how much it will cost, but whatever you think you can spare and you think will see me through will be ok. There are very few items I will need to pay for before graduation.

When I graduate, I hope to have some money left over, so I won't have to borrow too much from you then. I suggest you send the money by money-order, or send me a few blank checks and tell me how much I can use. We can cash any check for under $50, so use your own discretion.

There is one thing I do hope you have taken care of– that is my footlocker. The sooner I get that, the sooner I can get myself together. Besides, that's another thing we are supposed to have by Sunday.

It seems as though I have been bothering you a helluva lot lately, but I hope I can soon be on my own. Back in the days when I was in college I didn't mind too much when I needed money, but here I shouldn't have to be asking for any. I hope in about two weeks I'll cease bothering you.

And oh yes– before I forget, please make a dental appointment for me. I need a few fillings.

That's about all,

Love,

Herb

November 18, 1943

Dear Folks,

I am writing this letter from our laboratory, because I am listening to a rather dull lecture, and I thought I might as well spend my time profitably.

This morning, I went over to the clothier and got my final fit on clothing. As soon as it is altered, I can pick it up, and then I'll just have to wait for graduation. At this point, I do expect to graduate, but still we can't tell.

In the Army, each day brings in about 10 new rumors. One of today's worst is that we aren't going to get a furlough. This is purely rumor, but they have some good basis for it. It started due to the fact that they need us pretty badly now– which they didn't need about 4 weeks ago. Now, however, meteorologists are once again in great demand, so we may be shipped out at once.

Another thing is that we were told yesterday by one of our profs that they have found the best forecasters overseas to be the fellows who go over immediately after graduation. If this is so, and I am sent to a Port of Embarkation immediately, my changes for engineering school are very slim. I hope I can tell you more about this on Sunday, for if I can't come home, perhaps you can still make it up here for graduation. Time alone can tell. At present though, all indications point to a 10-day leave as we expect.

That's about all for now,

Love,

Herb

November 25, 1943

Dear Lou,

This is the last letter you shall receive from me as a Gadget [Cadet]. Monday I get said commission the AUS as a 2nd Looie [Lieutenant]. Tuesday, I shall arrive home for approximately 8 days (depends where I am sent).

Therefore, see if you can get home on the 4th-5th. Although officers aren't supposed to mingle with P.F.C.'s [private first class] or med students, we shall have to make an exception!

See you then,

Herb

November 26, 1943

From Headquarters Technical School

Army Air Forces Technical Training Command

Chanute Field, Illinois,

The following Avn Cadets AAFTTC Una sgd atchd 35th Tech Sch Sq 14th Tech Sch Gp AAFTTC, scd to grad fro Avn Cadet Meteorology Course TS AAFTTC Chanute Fld Ill on 29 Nov 1943, will be disch the av effective 28 Nov 1943 for the purpose of accepting commissions as 2D LTs AUS. By direction of the President they are ordered to AD effective 29 Nov 1943, are asgd Hq AAF Wea Wg Asheville N C, are placed on DS at this sta and art atchd 3th Tech Sch Sq 14th Tech Sch Gp AAFTTC. Offs will rank fr 29 Nov 1943:

Herbert Israel Barness, Warrington Pa. Cadet ASN: 13173461 Off ASN: 0874522

November 29, 1943

From: Technical School

Army Air Forces

Technical Training Command

Chanute Field, Illinois

Graduation Exercises

Aviation

Meteorological Cadets

Class 43-2

9:00 a.m.

Post Theater No. 1

Headquarters

Army Air Forces Central Technical Training Command

455 Lake Avenue

St. Louis (8), MO.

SUBJECT: Temporary Appointment

TO: Herbert Israel Barness,
Technical School, AAFTTC
Chanute Field, Illinois
A)   874522

1.   The Secretary of War has directed me to inform you that the President has appointed and commissioned you a temporary Second Lieutenant, Army of the United States, effective this date. Your serial number is shown after A above.

2.   This commission will continue in force during the pleasure of the President of the United States for the time being, and for the duration of the war and six months thereafter unless sooner terminated.

3.   There is included herewith a form for Oath of Office which you are requested to execute and return. The execution and return of the required oath of office constitute an acceptance of your appointment. No other evidence of acceptance is required.

4.   This letter should be retained by you as evidence of your appointment as no commissions will be issued during the war.

2nd Lt. Herbert Israel Barness asgd to 25th Wea Sq with Sta at New Castle AAF, Wilmington, Del.

December 1, 1943

Herb received birthday cards:

There's no ceiling on birthdays so keep 'em up. Defense needs are urgent and taxes still soar, While spending's restricted With rules by the score- But – wishes for Birthdays have pri*or*ity When the Birthday is yours and the wishes from me. (Kleins)

On Your Birthday in the Service.

Seein' how your birthday's due

You oughta celebrate,

But things a-bein' like they are,

Perhaps you'll have to wait;

But when the fightin's over

And you come home once more

We'll have a celebration

Like you've never seen before! (Silversteins, 813 S. 5th Street, Phila, 47, Pa.)

Another Birthday! Glory be! (with US flag)

So Let's keep em flying

Happy birthday! (Saffier cousins)

December 9, 1943

An Authorization for Allotment of Pay form, Herbert I. Barness, Army serial number 0-874522

Herb's current pay was discontinued because he went from Av. Cadet and received a commission to 2nd Lt. AC. His pay– $75 per month, indefinitely. The check was automatically deposited to Doylestown Trust Company to the credit of Joseph Barness, his father.

December 13, 1943

Typed on stationery from:

Ferrying Division

New Castle Army Air Base

Air Transport Command

2nd Ferrying Group

Dear Lou,

Sorry haven't written sooner, etc.

Well boy, here I am having an extended leave at the New Castle Army Air base (shall be referred to as NCAAB). This is my fifth day here and I find it quite enjoyable and interesting. The work is a snap thus far, and although I have been working every day, as yet I am not on a regular schedule. The boss comes back from an extended leave next Friday (the 17th), so I expect to be put to work shortly after that.

I shall attempt to give you a fair idea of this set-up before you get a chance to come out here next week.

We work here in an office, or group of offices, next to the operations office. Every plane that leaves this field must have a clearance from operations and weather before take-off, whether it be a training flight or over-seas hop. From this place we send out planes to every damn place in the world– and hope they get there. It is hard to write exactly what goes on here every day. Pilots come in by the dozen wanting clearances to a hundred different places. We forecast for them, fill out the necessary forms, give them a copy, and wish them luck--- then they are off.

Planes here come and go. Bombers, pursuits, trainers, liaison, and even helicopters come down here. Every new plane the U.S. has has been here on its way over, for this is the last stop to who knows where. I am not so keenly interesting in weather, the set-up here, or even being an officer, but I certainly enjoy talking to the pilots and looking over all the ships. It's all new to me, but even the fellows who have been here for several months are still thrilled by every new ship and pilot that comes here. A guy will come in and tell us what a helluva good time he had in Cairo last weekend; or the neat American nurse he met in India; the food he ate in China; the women in Australia; the weather in England, etc. And let me tell you boy, some of them have damn good stories. This is strictly a ferry command, and none of the boys see any action—but they do get close thrills.

An example of some of the work done is something like this: The Glenn Martin company will call up and say they have 15 bombers ready to ship out. The operations office will start calling the pilots in T.O.Q (Transient Officers Quarters) until they get 15 men or <u>women</u>.

They will hop into one of the two converted TWA Sleeper ships, either FUBAR or SNAFU. FUBAR is "Fucked up beyond all reality." Down to the Martin plant they go, and in about two hours they are back with a bunch of brand new B-26's. Boeing will call from California to send some men out---and out they go.

Last Friday night, FUBAR went down to Baltimore with a full load, had engine trouble, and had to come limping back on one engine, while all the passenger-pilots were shitting green.

This is also a transition school, WASP (formerly WAF) training center, and an Air Corps sub-supply depot.

In transition school they learn to fly any one of many ships, including the P-47, P-51, P-39, P-40, B-17, B-25, B-26. Also many men get instrument training and ratings here.

The WASPS [Women Airforce Service Pilots, the first women in history to fly America's military aircraft] are fair. They are a much higher caliber gal than the WACS, WAVES, SPARS, etc., but most of the ones I have met are pretty hardened and quite masculine. However the newer ones are damn nice, and retain their feminine complex. They are a great bunch of women, and I'm not kidding. They eat with us in the officers mess, have all privileges in the officers club, and what's more, their quarters are right next to our B.O.Q. [Bachelor Officers' Quarters]. I knew quite a bit about the WACS from experiences at Chanute, and also several WACS around here, but these WASPS have it all over them. They are nicer women, much neater, and much better looking. Of course, they have their share of bags.

I haven't mentioned it, but this is definitely an officers' field. Usually officers are in the minority at a post, but here there are about three officers to every enlisted man. The enlisted men here are only the absolutely essentials, whereas most of the officers (about 80%) are pilots who stay about a week, are instructors, or are in transition school.

From reading this letter, you shall probably gather that I am well impressed by this place-- well I am chum, but I know it won't last very long. When I see you I will be able to tell you more about it, and when you get here you will be able to see for yourself-- especially our shitty BOQ (BOQs are about the worst thing here.) (There are about 10 different BOQs here including 3 WASP quarters, which are similar to ours).

See you out here soon,

Best of luck,

Herb

In pen:

Lt. H. Barness

Base Weather Station

NCAAB

Wilmington, Delaware

P.S. I get my mail here at the office.

P.P.S. They have a radio here so we are always happy while we work.

CHAPTER 5

1944

OVERSEAS DUTY

1944 was a year of travel and getting closer to the war. In January, Second Lieutenant Herbert Barness was relocated from New Castle AA Field, Wilmington, Delaware, and assigned to Army Airways Communications System Wing, Selfridge Field, Michigan, for more course work and training.

In March, he was assigned to the 2nd Overseas Processing Squadron AACS at McClellan Field, California, where he awaited further orders. In April, he was made a Commanding Officer of a group of "well over 100 men." At this point, he knew where he was going next. He arrived in Oahu, Hawaii in May and was appointed Weather Liaison Officer. He was the youngest officer in the Squadron, and he had the opportunity to travel to other islands.

January 7, 1944

Typed on Ferrying Division stationery

Dear Lou,

Although you are long overdue in writing, the folks have been constantly begging me to write to you. Here goes.

This past week has been exceptionally tough on me. Last Sunday afternoon I worked for Davison who wanted to spend the rest of the day doing other things. For this, he offered to work for me on Monday, when I had five hours work. Tuesday, I was to be on research, but my roommate has taken over this job exclusively, so I had off. Wednesday I had off, but did some special work for about 5 hours Wednesday night, for which I got Thursday off. Today, Friday, I had off the entire day, because I am now on the 19-hour shift.

Well, since I had nothing in particular to do at home all week, and I didn't feel like getting drunk all the time, I was an eager beaver, so I worked every day from 0730 EWT to 14, 14, 16, or 1700 every day except today. This was one of the smartest things I ever did since I have been in the Army, although there is an old saying that one should never volunteer for anything in the Army.

We had P.P. (Pretty Poor) weather from Monday until Thursday, so instead of writing many clearances during these days (until noon on Thursday), I spent the time fooling around with the pilots who were in the office from 0700 EWT until all hours of the night waiting for this field to open up. Also all routes North and South were closed.

Instead of just giving them the straight weather here, as usual I gave them the weather they wanted. If they wanted to fly, they, themselves, knew whether they could handle heavy icing above 3000 feet, what visibilities they wanted, etc... Well, it isn't the general policy of the weathermen to give pilots the pilots' conditions. The first lieutenant wasn't in very much, but if he were he probably would have given me hell. I wasn't officially on duty all week, so the other forecasters on charge would just tell me to take all doubtful cases, after they would tell the pilots the true facts. The boys around here in the weather office are a damn nice bunch of guys, but they worry too much, as it should be—I guess, about getting hell from somebody.

As a result of this, I had one helluva good time and made many many friends. When I would go to lunch, pilots would come down to the mess hall, offer to buy me everything, if I would just hurry and get back to the weather office. Thursday morning I was going to sleep late after working late Wednesday night, but at 0815 EWT I was awakened by three pilots telling me I promised them 2 miles visibility in the morning. When I got to the station, the visibility lifted to 2 miles. Today, those three pilots and crews are in Africa.

My only close call was very interesting. Some hot pilot landed in here on Tuesday night at 1655 EWT in a P-38. He was headed for Newark, where they take all pursuit ships, crate them, and ship them over. Pursuit ships are not ferried across, because they don't have the gas load.

Well, this fellow was bringing the plane in from the factory down south, and he wanted to get to Newark in a bad way. His home was in Dallas; as soon as he made this delivery, he had an eight-day leave, and his wife was expecting a baby on Wednesday.

Operations didn't want to clear him, because as I told you, the ATC cannot make deliveries after sundown. It would only take him about 15 minutes to get to Newark, but it would take at least 15 minutes here before he would be allowed to leave. Sunset being at 1717 EWT, operations said nix.

He came in the weather station, and asked how the weather would be n Wednesday. I told him it would be P.P. (Pretty Poor). He told me his story, and asked if I would sign his entire clearance. Well, I am only a shavetail [a newly commissioned officer]; I don't have much chance for promotion as long as I am in weather, so I gave him a full clearance to Newark. By this time, it was 1700 EWT. However, once I cleared him, operations didn't say a damn thing, because it was my responsibility until he landed safely at Newark.

He hopped into his plane, taxied out to the runway, and just as the tower gave him the O.K. on his take-off, Newark called in and said we absolutely shouldn't send anyone up there, because they had ice on the runways, and they were putting salt on the runways. Immediately I grabbed the interphone system in operations and yelled: "P-38 flight to Newark cancelled—get the hell in here." He came back.

Well, that's about all new around here now—oh yes, I borrowed one of the boys' cars (a corporal friend of mine here in the office) and went down to see Gene Sunshine today.

Sustineo Alas,

Herb

Printed:

P.S. This letter was written on the 7th. The P-38 pilot got to Newark the next day on a closed field. When he got back to Dallas, he was the father of a baby boy– have seen the old man since.

January 11, 1944

From: Regional Control Office

25th Weather Region

Lynbrook, Long Island, New York

Reassignment of Weather Officers to Army Airways Communications System Wing 7 January 1944

2nd LT HERBERT I BARNESS O874522, AC RELD fro New Castle AAFld, Wilmington, Del., assigned to Army Airways Communications System Wing, Selfridge Field, Mich.

January 17, 1944

On Joseph Barness Realtor-Builder stationery: Homes Built to Order on Desired Acreage

Dear Lou,

Haven't written sooner for many reasons, foremost of which is that I did not know your address??

Please excuse the lousy typing that you shall see, for I am used to typing on a teletype-standard keyboard.

As you may have heard by now, I am no longer stationed at NCAAB. I am not longer a weather officer, but since January 7 have been as AACS officer (Army Airways Communication System).

I don't know exactly what the AACS officer does, just as I did not know what a metro officer did until I got out in the field and actually performed my duties. However, I do know that the AACS officer is the tower officer, and is responsible for the landings and take-offs of every ship that comes to or from a field. Also, we must keep in contact with each plane until it reaches its destination.

I shall not attempt to tell you that this is the most important job on a field, because I learned long ago that no one job connected with flying in the AIR CORPS is the most important job. We work as a team, and without one, the other cannot operate. As you once told me, I may be only a small cog in the wheel, but the wheel cannot run without all the cogs.

Weather was quite interesting and I probably would have been satisfied with it if I thought I had any chance of advancement in it, but the outlook was very dark, since there are approximately 5000 too many weather officers. Even if this new job does not offer any more opportunities, it does offer a three-months' course in Radio, and gives me just a little more education. If it is at all possible, I do hope to get into something whereby I can use both my full knowledge of weather, plus my future learning of Communications.

I could not get any leave from NCAAB because I owe the Army 5 days from my last leave. You see, officers are allowed 2 ½ days a month leave, I have been an officer for approximately two months which means that I still have to pay back 5 days from my first leave of 10 days. Well, I went to see the Adjutant and told him it was OK with me if I owed then 15 days, just so I could get 10 days more now. What the hell, I'll be in the Army long enough to pay them back. Anyhow, he said no.

I told my first looey that, so he said I should take off a week, and if anybody wanted to know where I am, each day was my day off. It was damn nice of him to do this, but I knew I was in solid with that guy. In fact: as soon as I got my orders and he read them, he tried to talk me into staying here at NCAAB. However, I wanted this new opportunity, whether it be good or bad, so I told him I was going.

Already we have had two parties for me, and as soon as I go back next week, several more are scheduled. Some of our parties sometimes turn into orgies after several hours.

If you want me to drop any of the fellows a card from NCAAB or Michigan, Just let me know. Oh yes, I am going to Selfridge Field, somewhere close to Detroit. That's the field where a Colonel shot a colored fellow; a Lieut-Colonel embezzled funds; a Major accepted some bribes; and it happens to be the only Army field in the United States that is endowed. A Mr. Henry Ford endowed the field, and from what I hear, it is damn nice.

That's all,

Herb

Lt. Herbert I. Barness, A.C.

31 January 1944

From: Headquarters Army Air Base

Selfridge Field, Michigan

Special Orders:

2nd LT 8219 Herbert I. Barness 0874522 will report to CO, Det 2nd Airways Com Sq, for dy [duty]

February 1, 1944

Herbert I Barness

Report of Physical Exam

Selfridge Field, Michigan

Last smallpox vaccination 4/14/43

Tetanus 12/21/43

Appendectomy 1936. Appendectomy scar

Tonsillectomy and adenoidectomy 1940

Fractured left humerus 1938

Right eye 20/80

Left eye 20/60

Height 71 ¾ inches

Weight 172 pounds

February 1, 1944

Stationery says Selfridge Field, Michigan and has an insignia and picture of an airplane on it.

Dear Lou,

Greetings from the snow covered lands of Michigan. I am writing this letter as I sit on my bed in BOQ, overlooking beautiful Lake Michigan.

This BOQ is much better than the last. It is a frame building, steam heated– I have a corner room with two windows. Remember how close we were to the WASPS? Well, cut that distance in half and divide it by 2, and there is the WACS barracks. They are all enlisted personnel– pretty damn hard up because the flying personnel on this field is all colored. [When I knew him, Herb was absolutely not bigoted in the least. All I can imagine is that this was just the times...] There are a few white enlisted men here, but most of the whites are WACS.

My course here begins on Friday, and instead of lasting 3 months, will probably last 3 weeks, then overseas. I haven't told the folks that it is only 3 weeks for I'm not sure yet, but I do know that at the completion of this course I am going to take a boat ride.

Must go eat now,

Herb

February 3, 1944

Dear Folks,

Classes start today. We have two shifts here, and each week we shall alternate shifts. For the remainder of the week I am on the morning shift, that is 9 a.m. till 12 noon. Next week I go to class from 1:30 p.m. till 4:30. Very easy schedule– gym 3 hours a week, and code classes to begin soon. Therefore, at present, we go to school 6 days a week, 3 hours a day.

This course is over in about 4 weeks (or less) so I shall soon be on my way again. No chance of washing out since we are going to stay in weather and communications.

Saw "Lifeboat" last night– it was pretty good. Think I did tell you we saw the play "Life with Father."

Saturday I (and several others) expect to see the play "Janie." Then next week we shall see "Doughgirls." Also the picture "Madame Curie" will be on the field. The plays we see in the theatres in Detroit.

I am still spending money wildly since I now know I have a maximum of 2 months in this country. All the fellows, like myself, are anxious to get over, so we are all having our last fling.

Love,

Herb

P.S. Lunches in the officers mess cost 50 cents.

Suppers in the officers mess cost $1.00.

February 9, 1944

Dear Folks,

Received a <u>Christmas</u> present from Blooms yesterday. I don't know where it got lost in the mail, but I just received it. I shall probably write to them tomorrow.

We were walking around the field this morning, and we found this place is really a country club. The field is located just off a lake, in fact my barracks is about 50 feet from the lake. They have a boathouse here with quite a few small, and many large, boats for the use of the personnel. However, at present the lake is frozen.

Expect to be here until the end of February– no later. Haven't even unpacked my footlocker. If I get home between change of stations, I'll bring back about a half dozen bottles of "Canadian Club." Haven't been doing much drinking here, but am enjoying the finer things such as music, plays, and movies before going overseas.

Love,

Herb

February 11, 1944

Dear Lou,

They are working us to hell out here. Instead of the usual 3 hours a day of classes, we have to take an extra 1½ hours of code. This means I have to get to be by 3 a.m. because I have to get up at 0830.

This week, due to a very sore throat and cold, I haven't gone in to Detroit yet. Instead, last night and Tuesday night I spent the evening in the WACS barracks. The WACS here are quite different from the WACS at Chanute, and the WASPS at NCAAB. The WASPS, of course, have it all over any damn WACS, WAVES, SPARS, etc.

Comparing the WACS at Chanute and Selfridge, however, the WACS here are much better looking, and carry the well know Air Corps pride. Their intelligence, or rather their educational background, is about equal to a high school senior, or perhaps a year or two of college.

On Tuesday evening I met a beautiful WAC– just about as nice a girl as I ever did see. She was/is the kind of gal I would like to marry someday, although I have no designs on this WAC for several reasons. First of all– Religion. Secondly, she is a little too old for me.

Before you get into the Army as a Doctor, you better know how to handle Nurses. Nurses are the hottest thing on two feet when they are in the Army (and outside too). They are, for the greatest part, second lieutenants, and therefore spend most of their time in the officers club. I never bother with them because I know right from the beginning that they are too old for me (22 or 23)! But you better keep on your toes chum. [Herb had turned 20 on December 1, 1943.]

So much for wimmen.

I have 2½ more weeks here, and then shall be sent to a processing center. At the processing center, I shall get all necessary shots (including boosters), check my teeth, get an issue of field equipment and clothing, crawl on my stomach under live machine-gun fire, and qualify again with pistol, rifle, etc. From there…

So long,

Herb

February 19, 1944

Dear Lou,

How is the weather in Boston? This goddamn Michigan weather is a pain in the rosey red. Every night it snows, and every day it is colder than hell. I shall be very glad to get to Tennessee or California in three weeks.

I don't think I ever told you what we have been taking here, and I am quite sure I told no one else. Although, at present, our work is not of a "secret" nature, it is confidential. If you will read Army Regulation 380-5, page 4, paragraph 4- sections (a), (b), and (d), [Department of the Army Information Security Program discusses safeguarding and protection information, and this appears to be related to controlled, unclassified information and access for official use only] you will not ask any questions, because I won't give any answers.

I will tell you this, however, our training is highly technical, practical, and some administrative work. With these three leads, you may (?) be able to tell what I am doing. If I write you a letter from Germany in two months, don't be surprised; although I may also get stuck somewhere in the U.S.A. Do not think that I am going to the European Theater because I mentioned Germany. I can just as easily (or probably) go to the Pacific.

I don't know if I will get a delay before going to a P.O.E., but if I do, I'll be up to see you and "rack-back" those "campus commando" pals of yours!! If possible, I would rather come up to see you than your coming home to see me.

By the way, we sent Mom a dozen roses for Valentine's Day. If I get any time off to get home, I'm going to take Pop a few bottles of "Canadian Club."

I am spending my dough very very freely, and I don't give a shit– as usual.

Will probably see you in two weeks.

Best of luck,

Herb

TO ANSWER YOUR QUESTIONS:

(1) Am in one swell outfit– much much better than weather.

(2) To go from 2nd to 1st LT., must have 6 months in grade in the U.S.A., or 3 months overseas. Things are very stable now, so I probably won't make 1st before May or June.

February 27, 1944

Dear Lou,

In case you ever get around to it, you better write before next week because we are going to be leaving this place around the 4th or 5th. I shall send you my new address as soon as I get it.

I was going to send you my "last will and testament" and "Power of Attorney," but I think I shall send it directly home. You were going to be the recipient so that the folks wouldn't take it too bad. However, I think I shall let them get it because they are getting broken in to the idea of my going overseas.

The work here is very very interesting, and like the whole set-up much better than weather. Pretty soon I hope they put me in business for myself on some beautiful south sea island.

Just received your letter as I start this side of the page. To sum up your letter, or rather to answer any questions, I have never thought seriously of marriage, and I am sure I won't do so for the duration plus six months.

Went to Chicago last weekend and picked up about ½ dozen bottles of "Canadian Club" to take overseas with me.

During my stay here at Selfridge, I have really raised royal hell. I have been to every hotel, bar, night club, theater, and have seen every woman, play, movie, dance band (T. Dorsey and Gene Krupa, Vaughn Monroe, Glen Gray) in the whole city of Detroit. I called up the star of the show "Doughgirls" for a date, but was unsuccessful. Such is life. If you are ever in Detroit, I can give you some good addresses– all kinds of women!

Pay Day next Tuesday, and as usual I am broke. I'll have to ask for a raise in a few months.

Best of luck,
Herb

P.S. Have no idea if and when I will be home

March 4, 1944

From: Headquarters,

Second Airways Communications Squadron

Army Airways Communications System Wing

AAF

Suite 1920

33 North LaSalle Street

Chicago 2, Illinois

2nd Lt. Herbert I Barness released from assignment and assigned to 2d Overseas Processing Sq AACS McClellan Field, Calif.

Each O is atzd 10 day delay en route.

Subject: Clearance. Herb transferred from Selfridge Field, Michigan, to McClennan Field, California. Transferred from 2nd A.A.C.S., Det.

Herbert I. Barness, 2nd Lt., A.C. 0-874522

20 March 1944 to 14 April 1944.

March 21, 1944

On parchment paper (copied in duplicate)

Return address: Lt. H Barness

McClellan Field

Sacramento, Calif.

6-cent air mail stamp

Dear Folks,

It is 9 p.m. here, or midnight back East where you are. I am writing this letter in duplicate, one for home and one for Lewis.

My trip was very interesting and enjoyable, and I shall try to tell you the high points of it.

From Phila. to Chicago, it was very dull, and not particularly comfortable riding via coach. My partner was a sailor coming home after a year at sea.

In Chicago I met my twin [Have no idea what this means!] and we went to see Uncle George. He was in bed and his nurse didn't want us to see him. Before going out there, I called Aunt Rose and she had to be in town so I never did see her. Ruth came over while we were at the apartment. She was with her son, Jeff, who is in the fourth grade in school.

Ruth was very nice, and after awhile, she brought out a bottle of brandy about 100 years old– good stuff. We talked about the family, and she told me about their family. Before I left, I went in to see Uncle George. He is much better than he was 4 weeks ago, but he can hardly talk. He had some sort of blood clot in the brain– Lewis would probably know what it was.

My observations of their whole set-up is that they now have twice as much money as they know how to use. I thought Orleans had plenty of money, and Pat had lots of connections, but the

Lapins are definitely society people. Their furniture and setting is beautiful. I was very favorably impressed, and so was my twin.

Left Chicago 8:15 Friday night. I had upper-eight, and a 1st Looie Doctor had lower-eight. My twin had upper-seven. That's all I knew when I went to bed at 9 p.m.

The next day we met the rest of the people in our car. There were three women with children (2 year olds) going to the coast to their husbands in service. There was another doctor– a captain. Two commanders in the Navy, 3 Ensigns, and two Waves– an Ensign and a Lieutenant j.g. (same as a 1st Lt.). The rest were civilians.

Saturday morning we (the two doctors and us) played pinochle for several hours. We usually stopped at a town about every two hours, so we went out and got some air. In the afternoon we played with the kids, talked, and raised hell. Our car was the last on the train, so we had a parlor car on the back half, and an observation platform.

Saturday night we stopped in Cheyenne, and the 4 of us (2 doctors and us) went in to town and got a few drinks (we were there for ½ hour). We came back and the Army and Navy members of our car had a swell time talking, and everyone but me was drinking. If you remember I wasn't feeling well when I left home, and the Doctors told me not to eat too much or drink.

Sunday morning we stopped in Ogden, Utah, for 2 hours, so we ate breakfast in a hotel there. It was in Ogden that I saw my first mountains– and they are mountains.

From there we went on the Great Salt Lake for 38 miles, and with a mountainous background, it was very beautiful.

I ripped my hanger on my blouse, so the WAVE lieutenant j.g. sewed it for me.

Sunday night everyone was singing, drinking, and having a wonderful time in the observation car.

THEN WE ARRIVE IN SACRAMENTO AT 5:20 a.m.

We went to a hotel, got a room, and slept till noon. Sacramento is the capitol of California, so it is full of politicians.

I checked in today and find that I have completed everything. Therefore I am only waiting for orders here, and shall do a lot of sightseeing and hell-raising.

Will write more later,

Love,

Herb

March 25, 1944

Dear Folks,

Still here waiting for my papers to come thru. At present I am sitting in the Red Cross Canteen waiting for a plane ride to San Francisco.

My life here is the best yet. Beautiful weather, the most beautiful field I have ever seen, and absolutely no work. All we do is eat, sleep, drink, and be merry. It is wonderful– but expensive. This is a vacation that is a vacation. If I can get a plane ride to Mountain Home, I'm going up to see Marvin. However, I don't think Marvin will be there for very long any more.

Please send, or have sent, my sunglasses immediately by special-delivery airmail!! This is a land of sunshine, and I could use those glasses.

I received the pictures I took in Detroit. I shall send them to you as soon as possible.

That's all,

Love,

Herb

March 27, 1944

Stationery says Officers' Club, McClellan Field, California and has an 8 cents airmail stamp

Dear Folks,

This place is certainly the nicest I have ever been at. Everything is perfect around here.

I got sunburned the other day, which makes me laugh when I think of how the weather was at home. We never wear coats or any heavy clothing here at all.

This evening, as every Sunday evening, there was a buffet supper in the officers' mess. We had turkey, peas, carrots, Jello fruit salad, potato salad, mashed potatoes, ham, radishes, skunions, olives, shrimp, milk, coffee or tea, ice cream, and cake for dessert. There were several other courses to the meal that I didn't eat. During the meal, there was an orchestra playing classical and popular music and the setting was perfect. I only wish you would come out here to take a look at this place! Can't describe how lovely the whole set-up is.

Boy, I'm crazy about it here. I wouldn't mind being stationed here permanently after coming back from overseas.

By the way, all the meals here are excellent, and all are very reasonable.

Please send my sunglasses immediately if you haven't already done so.

Oh yes, it seems funny, but yesterday, Saturday, we heard the opera from New York at 10:30 a.m. Tonight we heard [Walter] Winchell and Martin Dies at 6 p.m. whereas you heard them at 9 p.m.

That's about all,

Love,

Herb

March 27, 1944

Dear Lou,

Boy, what a picnic we are having out here! I am all through processing, and therefore have absolutely nothing to do but eat, sleep, drink, and be merry.

I got sunburned the other day when I was out running around the swimming pool in shorts.

On Saturdays, Sundays, and Wednesdays we have an orchestra playing while we eat. The food is excellent, and very reasonable.

Everything here is so perfect, I wouldn't mind being stationed here permanently after coming back from overseas.

I am going to Frisco on Wednesday, Los Angeles on Thursday or Friday, and if I can get a lift I am going up to Mt. Home next week. This, of course, is assuming my orders won't come for about two weeks. Wherever we go from here on our own (Los Angeles or Frisco), we can always hop a plane. It takes ½ hour to Frisco, and about three to Los A. Great stuff!!

I have been batting around as usual, only more so. On Friday night I had 4 different pre-arranged dates!! I finally called three of them off and went out with a General's daughter. She was pretty fair, but not too beautiful. She goes to UCLA.

I have been flying in a plane here that you probably never heard of, but soon shall. It's the P-61 "Black Widow" night fighter. It's a helluva sweet job.

That's about all for now,

Best of Luck,

Herb

P.S. Sonny is out at sea!!

April 3, 1944

Dear Folks,

Played golf every day last week, then on Friday went to San Francisco for the weekend.

We had a swell time there going to all the hotels and nightclubs. On Saturday afternoon, another fellow (not my twin) and myself, plus a third fellow and his wife, went out to the horse races.

We two single fellows shared all betting expenses, and together won $70, or $35 each. For the first, and last, time at the races, it wasn't bad.

On Sunday afternoon some man took us to his house to meet the family and have a few drinks. It was very funny, two of us were just walking down the street, and he picked us up. He has a son in the Air Corps so he wanted us to feel at home. It is rare to meet such swell people.

I received my glasses today in good shape.

It may interest you to know that I have been made commanding officer of a group of "well over 100 men." All these men are going over, and I am going to be responsible for them.

As a result of becoming commanding officer, I know where I am going, and when I am leaving. I have another officer as my adjutant.

Don't worry about where I shall be sent to because I will be in a pretty good spot. The Japs have been cleared out of there long ago, so there is nothing to worry about. In fact, the Japs never had a chance there.

My greatest responsibility is my squadron of men.

By the time you answer this letter, you will answer it to McClellan Field, but I shall probably be in a Port of Embarkation. Therefore, all out-going and in-coming mail is censored. All your letters, and all mine, will therefore be confined to family and personal matters rather than anything at all to do with the Army.

I hope you have gotten all the signatures for my Will and Power of Attorney, because I signed a statement saying it was taken care of.

That's all,

Love,

Herb

April 7, 1944

Dear Lou,

Having one helluva good time! All we do is play golf daily. Have done a little flying in some new ships. Saw a B-29 today!!

Expect to leave here soon for all points west. Having an easy time with my men so far. My headaches shall begin when I get to a P.O.E. [Point of Embarkation]

Best of luck,
Herb

April 11, 1944

From: Headquarters

McClellan Field, California

Future address: APO 16011A
C/o Postmaster
San Francisco, Calif.

April 11, 1944

From: Headquarters

Second Overseas Processing Squadron

Army Airways Communications System, AAP

McClellan Field, California

Special Order:

The following named O's… are directed to proceed to Camp Stoneman, Pittsburg, Calif. So as to arrive thereat during the daylight hrs of 15 Apr 44:

2nd Lt (0200) Barness, Herbert I.

April 16, 1944

From: Army Service Forces

Composite Command Group

Camp Stoneman, Pittsburgh, California

Certificate:

The undersigned Officer, hereby certifies that except for the roster of names listed below, all Officers and Enlisted Men of Code No. AF-121-A(6) have fired the basic weapon with which they are armed

April 20, 1944

Dear Lou,

If you ever get around to writing anyone, you may be interested in my address:

Lt. H. Barness
APO 16011-A c/o Postmaster
San Francisco, Calif.

I haven't written for some time due to the added work. Taking care of a bunch of men is a wee bit more difficult than a daily game of golf.

I don't think I have ever signed my name and rank as many times as I have signed since being in a squadron. My exec officer and I censor all of our outfit's mail, and I sign all passes, memorandum receipts, etc... It's a helluva lot of fun.

Don't ever say that nurses aren't the hottest things alive. Last night I had my first date on this place. She was a nurse shavetail, and brother those damn women sure are experienced. Need I say more!

While in Sacramento, I dated a civilian nurse several times, and she too was as hot as a firecracker. You are going to have a great time as soon as you graduate! Why in the hell I didn't take medicine instead of engineering I shall never know.

The reason for my name in the lower left hand corner is that I censor my own mail. The usual procedure for Enlisted Men's mail is to use a regular censor stamp and sign underneath. Officers' mail is censored individually, and may also be censored by the Base Censor.

Censoring Enlisted Men's mail is really very interesting, although sometimes boring. Reading all our men's mail is certainly an excellent way of reading the character of the man. All censorship is confidential, but we get some good ideas why they may bitch. As yet, however, we have had absolutely no bitching, so am very happy.

That's about all,

Best of Luck,

Herb

May 9, 1944

At Sea

From: Headquarters

U.S.A.T. "James H. Kinkaid"

Office of the Transport Commander

Debarkation Orders
Herb is on his way to Oahu.

May 12, 1944

Dear Folks,

Arrived safely here on the island of Oahu (pronounced Wahoo). This island is one of a group of 5 islands comprising what is generally known as Hawaii.

So you see, I am quite safe and shall continue to have a helluva good time. This is the island that had all the bombing on December 7, 1941, and although I cannot mention any military installations, you should know what field I am on.

I delivered all the men safely, and have been relieved of my job. However, I have a very very good position now, and things should work out very well.

Will write more tomorrow,

Love,

Herb

May 15, 1944

On paper-thin air mail stationery

Dear Folks,

Shall continue holding off that long letter until I find out my definite position. As things stand now, I am going to be a politician, or at least have a political job.

The climate out here is absolutely wonderful. Sun shines all day long, but it is a dry heat, and there is always a cool breeze. At night, one can always use a blanket.

Had a steak a few minutes ago (we can get steak anytime after 8 p.m.) and met 4 officers coming back from New Guinea. They saw the first WAC and first white woman they have seen in 2 years. There are few women on this place, which so far, is the only drawback.

That's all,

Love,

Herb

P.S. Sorry I couldn't call you on Mother's Day, but shall make up for it after the War. Was thinking about all at home today though.

May 15, 1944

Written on heavy paper, and it looks like it was typed on a special machine. It is all in caps, but I am not copying it that way here because it is difficult to read!

Dear Folks,

Finally getting around to writing everyone via carbon-copied letters. By this method, I think I can catch up on most of my delinquent correspondence.

After leaving the States, we had an uneventful voyage across the beautiful blue Pacific. The first day out, we hit some awful weather, which disturbed our internal systems. However, I was not a victim of seasickness, although I had one helluva headache for quite some time. I did not get the opportunity to feed the fish though.

Since I cannot tell you too much about the trip, let me refer you to the article in the issue of Readers Digest containing the story of "Troopship." The trip was not too pleasant, but it certainly could have been much worse. We saw flying fish, a whale, and many other species of fish. The Pacific was as blue as blue ink, and when the sun was shining, it was difficult to understand how Rickenbacker and his crew lasted for thirty days out there. The Pacific, as the name indicates, is the peaceful ocean.

Landing here on the island of Oahu (pronounced Wahoo) was the beginning of a new adventure. Oahu, if you shall look on a map, is one of the 5 islands comprising the Hawaiian Islands. Back in the states, or Mainland, we always referred to these islands as Hawaii, although Hawaii is one of the least populated of the group.

Oahu contains Honolulu, Waikiki Beach, and the field on which I am stationed (name not permitted) was very well known on December 7 [Hickam Airfield]. To make things difficult [part of sentence cut out by censors]. Directly in front of our house, on the street, there is a large bomb crater filled in with asphalt. Our house wasn't damaged very much except for a few cracks on the outside. The house next door, however, was completely demolished.

While mentioning our house, I might as well describe it to you. There are four lieutenants living in it. We have two bedrooms (two beds in each) bathroom (with shower and bathtub), living room, kitchen (complete with G.E. Frigidaire and Westinghouse Electric Range), breakfast nook, and a laundry room!!! Isn't this a helluva way to fight a war!!!

Nothing is rationed here except gasoline. Steak, fresh vegetables and fruit, canned goods, and everything in the food line is plentiful. A quart of liquor is worth its weight in gold, although beer, cokes, etc. are cheaper than in the States. On the field, prices are very reasonable, but in Honolulu things are sky high.

On Sunday, one of my roommates and I went in to Honolulu, and from there to Waikiki Beach. I have never in all my life, even in New York after all the shows let out, seen a city or beach so crowded as this place. Let me give you a few statistics of the island of Oahu:

There are approximately 350 service men to every <u>one</u> woman here. Now that can be broken up slightly. We can say there are 275 service men to every <u>white</u> woman on the island. You see, this place contains many Chinese, Japs, Hawaiians, and "Gooks" (Gooks are a combination of the three, or merely any one of the three.) Again we can break these odds down. One can say there are 3 officers to every white woman, so this puts an average shavetail way way down. However, for those of us who just came out this way, competition is just a keynote to success.

Well, it is almost eight o'clock here, and I feel like getting a steak, so must sign off.

Oh yes, must tell you whatever I can about my job. Not allowed to tell you exactly what I am doing, but in addition to other things, I have the ideal set-up of the war. I am my own boss, I have my own <u>office</u>, and really am putting to use my cadet training plus AACS training. I got rid of my squadron of men, but this job has them all beat. As far as promotions go, there are fellows here who have been shavetails for seventeen months. Looks like the grass is always greener on the other side of the street, or in this case, the ocean. When I was on the Mainland, we all thought the promotions were overseas; now everyone says the promotions are in the States. However, I am not worried in the least about promotions for I always wanted to get overseas, and the folks have nothing to worry about since I am quite safe. If they don't worry, it will make it much easier on them. This country is as much like to good old USA as any place imaginable– just one great big Florida. With my position now, I will be able to get close enough to the fighting lines if I so desire, or I shall be able to visit any of our islands out here.

Will write more when this masterpiece is answered,

Regards to all,

Herb

May 16, 1944

From: Army Air Forces

Headquarters 70ᵗʰ Army Airways Communications System Group

Office of the Group Commander

2ⁿᵈ Lieut HERBERT I. BARNESS, 0875=4522, AC, reld asgmt 145ᵗʰ AACS Sq, APT #953, & Asgd to Hq 70ᵗʰ AACS Gp, APO #953 and aptd Weather Liaison Officer (PD).

May 19, 1944

Dear Lou,

Hello there youngster. This is your old sea-going weather beaten brother. While you are taking it easy at HMS [assuming this is Harvard Medical School], I am out here fighting the war of Oahu for the good old USA. My best defense is the use of a mosquito net and some insect spray, but on "H" hour my lines are penetrated, resulting in a loss of a pint of blood per night.

Hawaii and Waikiki Beach are very lovely, but with so goddamn many GI's around here, and the sea-going Bell-hops, the place is too crowded. Walking through the streets of Honolulu, one can only see the Navy whites and the Army khakis. By the way, have you gone into khaki yet?

Before I forget, when do you expect to get your commission? I sent home my trench coat and short coat, so whenever you get that silver bar, that clothing is yours. I shall not need it for the duration plus 1000 years. Let me give you a little advice on other Army officers' clothing:

If you can, keep your raincoat and slap a few bars on it. This will save a little dough, and if necessary, you can have epaulets sewed on it. You can have my trench coat and short coat, which will save you about ninety bucks. Naturally, keep all underwear, socks, shoes, etc. If you are commissioned in September, do not buy any summer clothes, since you may never need any. Get yourself a blouse and pants, and two sets of pinks. Buy one garrison hat, and one overseas hat. That's all.

When you are about to get your commission, I shall send you a little advice on how to handle men in the Army, and I can really give you some good tips. You shall find that the medics are about the most hated outfit in the Army, but the Joes in the Air Corps have the most respect for the docs.

I don't expect to see you for quite some time, for there is a new ruling here in the Pacific that no man is entitled to a leave until he has served 24 months out here. If there is every anything urgent, cable me at the flowing address:

Lt. H. Barness

77th AACS AAF

AMCYDU APO 953

I shall be home in two days after arrival of any urgent message.

Well doc, shall try to send you some souvenirs after I get settled out here.

Best of luck,

Herb

May 22, 1944

Herb wrote to Bucknell University's Registrar, asking about obtaining college credit through extension courses in engineering, or whether he could receive credit towards his mechanical engineering degree for successfully completing the Army Air Force's Meteorology Cadet Course at Chanute Field. He wrote: This was a thirty-three week course, including such subjects as Dynamics, Synoptic Meteorology, Climatology, Map Analysis and Forecasting, etc. After completion of this course, I was a weather forecaster at New Castle Army Air Base, Wilmington, Delaware.

On the same date, he wrote to the Armed Forces Institute in Madison, Wisconsin, asking if they had any courses in mechanical engineering that he could study while situated on Oahu.

A reply was written to Herb on June 5, 1944, form the Office of Bucknell's Vice President, saying that the "Engineering faculty are going to grant a limited amount of credit toward a degree on work successfully done through the auspices of the Armed Forces Institute..." And also saying that "The Engineering professors do not feel that laboratory courses can be taken through the Armed Forces Institute."... and suggesting that if he wishes to take courses through the Armed Forces Institute, he should secure the approval, in advance, from the head of the Department of Mechanical Engineering.

Another reply was sent on Jun 12, 1944, from Bucknell's Office of the Dean. It read, in part:

Professor Reed [head of the Department of Mechanical Engineering], "writes me as follows:

"In reply to your note of June 5 concerning the correspondence from Mr. Barness, I wish to advise you that we could not allow him any credit for required courses in Mechanical Engineering for his work in Meteorology completed at Chanute Field. I do feel that this work might be substituted for certain electives in our M.E. curricula.

"Also we would allow him credit for any of our equivalent courses completed in the Armed Forces Institute, except laboratory courses."

May 26, 1944

Dear Folks,

Haven't received any mail from you at this address since I have been here. Did receive a V-mail letter from Lewis yesterday dated sometime in April.

Two nights ago, my roommates and I cooked our own dinner, which, no less, was a steak. We had some lettuce and tomato salad, corn, peas, soup, and crushed pineapples and peaches with ice cream. It was very good, so we shall probably try it more often.

Last night I was invited out to dinner in Honolulu. Another Second Lieutenant whom I met at McClennan was my roommate at the P.O.E., and was my adjutant of the Squadron, has been living here in Hawaii for the last fifteen years. When he went overseas, he went back to the States to go to Officer Candidate School, and then was assigned back here to his own home. He invited me to his home for dinner, and he also wanted me to meet his wife. He is thirty-six years old, has been married for the last ten years, has a beautiful home, but no children.

We had a very good home cooked meal, and for the first time since I have been here, I had some good bourbon. I have been invited there again, so after several years of living here, I should probably develop a second home.

Out of the shipment of my squadron of 120 men, I was the second youngest; and of all of the officers assigned to the 145th AACS Squadron, or the 70th AACS Group, or the 7th AACS Wing (which takes in one helluva lot of men), I happen to be the youngest officer. This offers no advantages, but may in the future offer some disadvantages. Some old guy with some rank will probably object to a young upstart getting ahead. I do look older than 20, so I keep my age pretty much to myself.

Well, I had to come all the way out to Hawaii to cut grass this year!! I cut our lawn in front of our house last week, and shall have to do the same this week. It's about one-third the size of our lawn at home, so I don't mind too much.

Several days ago in the officer's mess hall, we had corn-on-the-cob, fresh celery, and lots of fresh radishes. While you are just planting your garden at home, we are eating all the vegetables you shall get several months hence. This place has a wonderful climate so fruits and vegetables are always in season.

This afternoon, a captain (a pilot with 50 missions completed in the European theatre) and I went swimming. There is a very nice pool about a block from our house, here on the field. I expect to go swimming quite often, until I get too busy.

To answer Lewis's question, or statement, about GI's expecting a lot from the people after this war is over, let me say I am in full sympathy with these men.

Even though we, here, are far away from the actual fighting now, there is a different feeling toward the war here than there was in the States. The damn civilians in the States think that since there is rationing of food, shoes, liquor, and gasoline, and as long as they buy a War Bond every week, they are fighting the war. Out here in Hawaii, there is no rationing of foods or shoes, and they never had much liquor or gasoline, but they saw the war on December 7, 1941, and few of these people have forgotten. Lots of things happened here which were never told in the States, and perhaps you will never hear about, but we can see these things, and those boys shipped back to the States probably saw more than we.

There isn't a soldier, sailor, or marine here, no matter what rank, who isn't wishing that he was back in the States right now. Not necessarily at home, but just back in the States enjoying the gravy that the rest of the fellows who are the "Market Street Commandos" in service, and the defense workers who dodged the draft are having. We aren't a bitter bunch, and we wouldn't trade places with any 4F or defense worker, but we, like all damn humans, are jealous of what is going on in the States while we waste our time in the Army.

Take my own case, for example. I shall be a very poor example for the average GI, for, ever since I have been in the Army, I always had an ideal set-up. I enlisted as a cadet, came home every eleven weeks; was stationed at home for two months after being commissioned, wanted to get in Communications, so I got in; wanted to go to California, so was sent there; and finally wanted to go overseas, so was sent to beautiful Hawaii. However, through no fault of anyone in particular, all this has been a waste of time for me. I was taken out of college, thereby disrupting any plans I might have had, and also setting me back about 5 of the best years of my life.

After this war is over, I'm not going to sit and cry and complain about not getting any mercy as a veteran, but there are going to be very few monetary aids offered by the government that I shall refuse. Whatever little I do, I feel I am giving my share, and I'm out for all I can get.

Don't worry too much about my attitude for as you know, I really can't complain. I have a swell position here, associating with some damn worthwhile people, and enjoying myself as usual. Have met some nice women, so in a short while, my social life shall also be complete.

See you when the war is over,

Love,

Herb

May 29, 1944

Mailed with a six cents airmail stamp

Dear Folks and Lewis,

Sill haven't received any mail to this address, and if you will look at the envelope, you will see that I have changed my address. [70th AACS Gp, Apt #953, c/o postmaster, San Francisco, Calif]. Do not become alarmed, for I am still in the same place with the same set-up, but am now working right in headquarters.

My first address was "7th AAC," then "145th AACS Squadron," and now 70th AACS Group. You see, the Air Corps is broken up into "Wings," then "Groups," then Squadrons, etc. Well, as I told you previously, I have a good position, but until yesterday (Sunday), I was on trial, more or less, to see if I would make good at my job. I seemed to please them, so am now officially assigned to the Group, and my only boss is the commanding officer of the Group, who is a colonel. This still doesn't mean much as far as promotions go, but what the hell, I'm having a good time. As long as I don't mess up the works, I'll have a clear conscience holding my job.

By the way, exactly 6 months ago today, I was commissioned. I do hope to make 1st before Lewis though.

This afternoon, four other officers and I went out to Waikiki Beach to go swimming. We started for our pool here on the post, but they clean it every Monday, so we couldn't very well go swimming in an empty pool. Therefore, we called up our outfit, had them send down a command car and driver, and the five of us (plus driver) went down to the beach for a little swim.

It was the first time for all of us to be swimming at beautiful Waikiki, and all were rather disappointed. The beach was ok, but as one went into the water, the bottom was filled with coral. It was quite novel for swimming in the ocean, for after going in several feet, there was a slope downward forming a semi-swimming pool. The breakers are about 150 feet out from the shore. Next time we go, we are going to attempt to ride the surfboards in the breakers.

You might as well get used to the idea that you won't see me for the duration, but don't worry, as long as I am in business for myself, everything will be ok.

If you can, send me Booey's, Selma's, Connie's, Pat's, Marvin's and Gene's address [all cousins].

Hope you and Lewis don't mind me typing carbon copy letters to both of you, but I want to say the same thing, and am too lazy to rewrite two letters. If there are any objections, let me know, and I shall discontinue this practice. I only write to the two of you this way.

Love,
Herb

May 31, 1944

Dear Folks and Lewis,

Yesterday I had a little work to do at one of our outlying stations, so got myself a jeep and driver (officers are not allowed to drive off the post) and went up to do a little inspecting.

We drove by a lot of sugar cane field, and acres and acres of pineapples. My driver was a native of Hawaii, so he explained most of the surroundings to me. On our way back, naturally, was very anxious to pick a few pineapples. Although there is a fifty dollar fine for picking any (most of the fields belong to Dole Pineapple Company)—we came home with nine beautiful pineapples.

I put several in the Frigidaire to cool, sliced them when chilled, and ate to our hearts' content. They were as sweet as sugar, and really very delicious. The difference between eating fresh pineapples and those bought in the States is the same as eating fresh tomatoes from the garden and buying tomatoes a week old in the store.

I get as much work as I can finished in the morning, go for a short swim in the afternoon, and then work the rest of the afternoon and into the evening. Most of my work is paper work, good will, and handshaking. As I told you previously, a box of cigars and a case of liquor is necessary for this position, for I'm the guy that everybody comes to with their troubles, and I try to settle their minds. The usual procedure is for two opposing forces come to me, and I decide who will have to give in. Actually, I don't have anything to lose except for the fact that most of the men I deal with are Majors and above.

I suggest that the three of your get your pictures taken and send me copies at your earliest convenience. You already have mine, but I shall send you snapshots from time to time.

Love,
Herb

June 2, 1944

Dear Folks and Lewis.

Received your (from home) first letter to this address yesterday; and received a V-mail letter from Lewis address to my old APO number. We try to discourage V-Mail for they are too brief—take a hint Lewis.

After looking at Bud Thormann's address, I found out his location on this island. I tried calling him for about an hour today, then finally succeeded in contacting him. Sometime next week I shall get a Jeep and go over to his camp for some of my business anyhow, so I will be able to kill two birds with one stone.

Yesterday, four of the pilots living next door and I went on a tour of the island. I got my Hawaiian driver who knew all the spots of interest, thereby serving as a driver and guide. Two of the pilots have moving-picture cameras, and I constantly take pictures with Leonard's camera. I shall send you some of the pictures if I get any good shots.

It was a very interesting trip, going through most of Honolulu, and all of the surrounding country. Honolulu is like one big Coney Island (although I have never been to Coney Island—only heard about it) with all sorts of amusements and stands to sell the pre-war tourists everything from soup to grass skirts. Most of the stuff looks as though it has been made in the States and then sent over here.

The surrounding country, and beach, was very beautiful, although the Army, Navy, and Marines have done some work to their own advantage. In peacetime, this was probably a heavenly place to live.

If you want me to call some time, let me know about ten days in advance, so that I may make all necessary arrangements. I don't know how much it will cost, but shall probably be between twenty-five and thirty dollars. If you do decide you want me to call, in giving me the ten days' notice do not forget that it takes almost ten days for your letters to reach me. Also, we are five and one-half hours behind in time than you.

Love,
Herb

June 5, 1944

Dear Lou,

Haven't heard from you directly to this address yet. Let's get on the ball there Doctor.

Some of my old buddies are now stationed out here with me, so am very happy. It's always better gunning when two wolves are on the prowl, n'est pas.

No news around this place that I can tell you about. Will have to wait until the war is over to tell you my exciting times shooting the paper clips and rubber bands. Anyhow, will have to wait to tell you what little part I am doing in this great struggle for democracy—bullshit.

Read in the paper today that Rome is in the Allies' hands. Those poor guys in the Army must have a tough time of it, while we in the Air Corps sweat out this beautiful sunshine. My morale is quite high—higher than usual, but whenever I get to think about what I am fighting for, I have to think for one helluva long time. In the States it was quite glorious to be an officer with lots of wine, women and song. Overseas, it is slightly different, we don't frown upon civilians for we never see any, and we don't look for much glory. All we know is that this is war—and war is hell.

I hate war– Eleanor hates war– and Jimmie likes his piece too.

As we pulled out of San Francisco on the way over here, we passed under that wonderful engineering feat of the Golden Gate Bridge. As we did, the men kept saying" "Golden Gate in '48, Bread line in '49."

When I get back, I still hope to finish college, and then go into business with Dad– if he is still building.

Also when I get back, I expect to see you married, or very nearly married. How about it chum. Looks like you will have to produce the first grandchildren for the folks.

Aloha,
Herb

June 15, 1944

Dear Folks and Lewis.

Received three letters from home today, one from Lewis, and one from Bucknell. Two of your letters from home were written on the

5th and seventh, while Lewis' letter (a V mail) was written on the 30th of May. The mail service out here isn't too good, for until today, I didn't receive any mail since last Sunday. However, although mail is very important for everyone out here, there are other more important things coming this way that have priority on planes and shipping. I assume though, that the mail coming east is delivered much more satisfactorily.

The letter from Bucknell was just a reply to my letter asking about taking extension courses from the college. I expect, if possible, to take a few courses while out here. Don't know for sure if I will or not.

Received lots of news in all of your letters. Lewis wrote of Aunt Goldie expecting to marry again!! Quite a surprise!! Then there is Mary Todd's expecting a baby—how long ago did her husband leave for England??? Give her my best wishes.

From hearing all the news lately, it seems as though I may get home earlier than I expected I hope. Maybe we will clean up this whole mess before the end of 1945. Glad to hear of the B-29's bombing the hell out of Japan– a little dose of those 1000 plane raids that Germany suffered may get Japan to realize that we mean business. It always takes the Air Corps to put the other guys in their place.

Nothing new here of any other importance. Things are running as smoothly as possible.

As soon as I get the time, I am going to send Lewis my green shirts, trousers, and blouse. This will save him (you Lewis) one helluva lot of dough, and I don't expect to have the need for them for the duration. As long as I am stationed in the Pacific, the uniform is suntans thruout the year, and as you know, I shall be out here, someplace, for the duration. I shall leave the Air Corps patch on the blouse, hoping that Lewis will also be as fortunate as I in getting into the best outfit. Lewis, this should make it necessary for you to buy only one set of pinks, a hat, and as many summer uniforms as you find you need. You should already have both of my coats, and with the uniforms that follow you better not spend more than $100. I believe everything will fit, since we are almost of the same build (except of course I have one helluva lot more brawn). Do anything you wish in the way of altering the stuff.

[THERE IS A LINE CUT OUT BY CENSORS.]

That's all for now,

Love,

Herb

June 20, 1944

Dear Folks,

Nothing new here as usual.

You can send me Chick's sister's address– if she is fairly nice looking. Am going to look up Bud Thormann again this week.

Will send you some souvenirs of some of the islands closer to Japan as soon as I get time to pack them.

Had to interview some men today, which was exceedingly interesting. Have quite a position– would help me build and sell homes after the war!!

Love,

Herb

Am looking forward to coming home for Xmas.

June 22, 1944

Dear Lou,

Received your V mail of the 13th today.

What's the story on Harriet?

Have heard of Mary Todd's expecting– also Dorothy told me of her song. Suggest you write more often to keep up on the news!

I'm telling you lad– you better be getting married soon, or the folks are going to be disappointed! I'm going to be a bachelor for some time yet– as any fool can plainly see!

Am enjoying my job immensely. In fact, it is more of a racket than a job. I interview men, ride or fly around, sit behind a nice big desk, go give some bigshots hell, etc. I'm just eating it up! Shall send you some souvenirs of the islands of Tutuila, Bora Bora, Samoa, Kwajalein, Tarawa, etc., as soon as I get a chance to pack them.

Can't think of anything new to write,

Best of Luck,
Herb

Give Barnett my best wishes!

June 21, 1944

Dear Folks,

Received a V mail from Lewis today telling me of Harriet's announcing her engagement! What's the story– never knew she was going with anyone in particular. Makes me feel old to hear of the kids back home being grown up!

Very happy to hear of her engagement, which makes me think about things. She probably is going with some soldier, who, in peacetime, would just be another working boy. I have always felt, and it seemed as though everyone felt and looked upon me in the same like, as being a guy who always went in for the best– and nothing else. In other words, when I did things, I was pretty lucky to fall into some good thing and became a semi-"bigshot." I hope, and expect to do the same in civilian life. That is, if I go into building with you, we are going to be big and the best. None of that small time stuff!! Therefore, everything, including women– after the war, is going to be just so. Perhaps my plans shall have to change, but I am going to strive for perfection and be well known.

If you could only see the kind of job I have out here, you would see what I mean! I interview men, go on inspection trips, ride around, and sit behind a nice big desk. Quite a racket!

Nothing new around here– everything is going smoothly.

Love,

Herb

June 25, 1944

Dear Folks,

Sorry haven't written for the past two days– I try to write every other day, if possible.

Today, I have been feeling rather blue, for 3 of my old and very good friends have left. We had been together constantly since March of 1943, and except for the 2 months in New Castle, we were always at the same place and very close. Out here when we say good-bye, it is quite different than the usual farewell in the States. Therefore, I feel rather badly.

If I sit here and say good-bye to too many more fellows, I think I shall soon put in for a transfer to see some action. I shall probably feel better in several days, but right now I don't like it.

Nothing else to write,

Love,

Herb

June 30, 1944

Dear Folks,

Finally received a V mail from Lewis today.

I went on a complete trip around the island this morning and afternoon on an inspection trip of AACS installations. After going around the island about 6 times, one gets rather tired of it.

Did my last two months' allotment get to the bank? This month I have $100 allotted to the bank, so if I request anything, you can take my dough. Otherwise, if you have any use for it, naturally you are welcome to it.

I may need some money next month, for I expect to take several extension courses to complete college.

That's about all,

Love,

Herb

July 1, 1944

Dear Lou,

Received the uniforms yesterday. They were exactly what I wanted, and they fit quite well. Thanks very much. Can't say "would like to do the same for you" because I hope this damn war is over by the time you get out of internship.

Saw the best ball game I ever witnessed last Sunday. The 7th Air Force beat Navy, 4-0, in 12 innings. DiMaggio, McCormick, Dillinger, Lodigiani, and the whole gang played excellent ball. I get reserved seats to all 7th A.F. games, so miss very few of them. Keeps one's mind occupied, thereby allowing less time for reminiscing. I spend very few evenings at home– always out someplace.

Bob Hope, Francis Langford, and Jerry Colona are out here, so shall make an attempt to see them on Saturday.

Hope to hell you can keep out of the Army after the war is over. It isn't that the Army shall be too bad, but it will be a waste of time—at least from my angle.

If you have the opportunity, don't forget to see "Oklahoma," and the picture "A Guy Named Joe."

Best of Luck

Herb

THANX AGAIN FOR UNIFORMS!

July 7, 1944

From: Army Air Forces

Army Airways Communications System

HQ, 70th AACS Group

Special Orders:

2nd Lieut HERBERT I. BARNESS, 0874522, AC, (0200), 70th AACS Gp, AAF, APO #953, is aptd Gp Claims O. Auth to act as Board of one O in any case within the provisions of AW 105. He will, unless in the specific case a board of more than one O is required by statute, also constitute the investigating O, board of Os, or surveying O required by AR for the investigation of: (1) any accident involving death, personal injury, or property loss or damage within the jurisdiction of this Gp; (2) any other matter or incident, the investigation of which is ordered or required by proper auth.

July 13, 1944

Dear Folks,

Looks as though all of Saipan is now ours. This is just another stepping stone to Japan, and the end of the war.

These islands in the Pacific never meant much to me back in the States– in fact I never had much of an idea where any of them were. Since being out here, it is quite different though– we follow each move of the Armed Forces from hill to hill. After the war I certainly am going to have some good stories to tell you.

I think that I shall probably write V mail letters hereafter, for I cannot think of too much new to write from day to day.

I received several pictures from Harriet, which were taken back in Warrington in March. You have undoubtedly seen them. I would appreciate it very much if both of you would have your photographs taken, and also have Lewis's photo, and send them to me. This is the second time I asked you, and I don't want to nag you like you had to nag me to have mine taken!!! I shall be expecting them in the very near future.

Don't worry about me fretting when some of my old friends leave. It is just a temporary condition, for as one goes from place to place, one makes new friends. I have been monkeying around with these three swell fellows since I arrived here. In fact, we all arrived within the same week. One of them is the Captain with 50 missions over Germany. All are great guys.

That's about all,

Love,

Herb

July 21, 1944

By V Mail [Wikipedia: V-mail, short for Victory Mail, was a hybrid mail process used during the Second World War in America

as the primary and secure method to correspond with soldiers sta-
tioned abroad. To reduce the cost of transferring an original letter
through the military postal system, a V-mail letter would be cen-
sored, copied to film, and printed back to paper upon arrival at its
destination.]

Dear Folks,

Received 2 old letters from you, and 1 old V mail from Lewis.

Saw the 7th Air Force beat some local team in baseball. With the team
the Air Force has, very few teams beat us.

Haven't been doing anything exceptional, so there isn't too much to
write about. Believe you know just about what I do, therefore won't say
very much of it. Am still doing, and probably always shall do, a lot of
travelling.

You can subscribe to the Intelligencer for me if you will, and also to
LIFE magazine. Most magazines arrive here quite late, unless one has a
subscription– or so it seems.

Things are looking up all over the world, except back in
the States. Looks like I'll get a chance not to vote for Roosevelt
in 1944!!

Can't think of anything else to write,

Love,

Herb

July 23, 1944

By V mail

Dear Folks,

Received the clipping of Tom Stringer, and shall try to look him up very
soon. I still never have seen Bud Thormann.

Just heard that we are taking Tinian Island. This is good news for it indicates we shall probably take all of the Marianas. From there, it is just a matter of time before Japan sees it's a hopeless case.

The news from the other side sounds very encouraging. Perhaps Germany shall quit sooner than expected. If so, Japan might as well quit also.

Shall put off the telephone call until Lewis comes home in September. Time out here means very little, since we are all "sweating" out the end of the war and not day by day happenings.

Love,

Herb

July 31, 1944

There was a small piece of paper in this envelope with the following typed message:

This communication was delayed by the Military Censor for security reasons.

Dear Folks,

Mail, during this past week, was very erratic. For seven days, I did not receive a letter– then one day I got 9, and the next day 7! So I am slightly behind in my correspondence.

Do not worry if you do not hear from me for a little while off and on, for as you know, I am usually here and there, and everywhere. I have almost convinced myself that after the war I shall just continue to travel and never settle down. If I do settle down, I shall undoubtedly go into construction work.

At long last, tomorrow I am having my clothes, and souvenirs, wrapped and shipped to you. I have been delaying it unintentionally–

just never got around to packing the stuff. Of course, all of the clothes are at Lewis's disposal. Looks as though he shall get his silver bars before I do!

Since Lou graduates on the 25th, I shall call sometime around the 30th, if this is satisfactory. Let me know.

I expect to discontinue all allotment– except my insurance, beginning this month. There are several reasons for this, the main one of which being that I shall need some money for September 25; and another is that Christmas actually isn't too far off.

The 7th AAF certainly has the best ball club out here. It seems quite obvious that our team could easily bomb the hell out of any, and all, the major league clubs on the Mainland.

I expect to see Tom Stringer again this week. We shall probably eat together some evening, and then see a ball game.

On Saturday, I saw your buddy– Franklin D. Roosevelt. He was out here– probably looking for some votes!!

At the time General MacArthur arrived here, I was present in the Control Tower. He wore that famous "Hat" and "Jacket" that he always uses. Seems as though all the big boys were on this field a short while ago.

Love,

Herb

August 10, 1944

Dear Lou,

Received your immense stack of letters– one V mail from about 2 weeks ago.

Hope you can get me the clothes ok. I have sent my stuff home, so you can look for it in about 3 weeks.

Things out here are about the same as usual, with only slight variations, which one cannot write about. Am enjoying my work immensely, but am looking forward to getting a little excitement. It's ok having a nice soft job, but what the hell, I might as well do whatever I can before the war is over.

A met a S/SGT in my outfit today, with whom I went to high school. His name is Constantine– don't know if you know him. Johnny Miller and Doug Axenroth are also out here. Am going to see them all on Sunday. Being the only officer from the Bucks [County, PA] gang, I shall have to supply them with liquor, for only officers can get liquor here.

Well Lou, let me hear from you.

Best of Luck,
Herb

August 23, 1944

By V mail

Dear Folks,

Received three letters from you yesterday, which were written from August 4 to the 12th. It seems as though the mail is being delayed, but only the transportation problem can be blamed.

Glad to hear you sold the truck, at last. As soon as the war is over, am sure we will again need many more. Still hope to go to Europe to build.

How are things at home? Everything out here is as usual, and things are going great.

Love,
Herb

September 3, 1944

From: Army Air Forces

Army Airways Communications System

HQ, 70th AACS Group

Special Orders:

2nd Lt. HERBERT I. BARNESS, 0874522, AC, (0200), Hq, 70th AACS
Gp, AAF, APO #953, is aptd Group Morale and Special Services Officer
(AD).

September 3, 1944

Dear Folks,

This is the 3rd letter I am writing you in which I shall try to tell you CUT
BY CENSOR. The other 2 letters were returned by the censor.

By the time you receive this, Lewis should be home. It really must feel
good to have him home after 7 years of college. I must say that it would
be quite wonderful if both of us could be home, but that day shall come in
the near future.

I don't know what his status is– is he Dr. Barness– or Lt. Barness?
Whichever it may be, he has been sweating it out a long time.

There isn't anything particularly new here. We have begun thinking
that it shall soon be fall in the East, although the climate here never
changes.

The homes here are all built without any heat– it isn't necessary. I have
yet to see a house with a cellar, and any home below $10,000 doesn't even
have a foundation. This entire island is volcanic, and after many years it has
become extremely rocky and hard. I shall send you some advertisements

of homes when I think of it– they seem ridiculous. The prices are about 3 times that of the States.

Love,

Herb

September 5, 1944

From: Commanding Officer, 91ˢᵗ Army Air Forces Base Unit, APO 953, c/o Postmaster, San Francisco, California.

The records of this office show that Second Lieutenant Herbert I. Barness, Air Corps, O-874522, is assigned to 91ˢᵗ Army Air Forces Base Unit. By order of the Secretary of War.

September 14, 1944

From: Army Air Forces

Army Airways Communications System

HQ, 70ᵗʰ AACS Group

Subject: Travel Orders

2ⁿᵈ Lt HERBERT I. Barness, o874522, AC, (0200), 70ᵗʰ AACS Grp, AAF, APO #953, not on tem dy Det #35, APO #240, WP from APO #240 by first avail mil ap to Det #28, APO #241, Det #32, APO #244 and Det #33, APO #246, reporting upon arr to the OIC thereat, for the purpose of coordinating AACS Weather activities thereat, and upon comp of tem dy, he will return by first avail mil ap to his proper sta. Baggage alws of sixty-five (65) lbs while traveling by air is auth...

September 16, 1944

Article in Doylestown Intelligencer newspaper titled, "Lieut. Barness Tells About 'Bull Session' In Hawaii"

"Recently a reunion "Bull session" in the Hawaiian Islands was enjoyed by seven servicemen from Doylestown and vicinity, according to a letter form Lt. H.I.Barness, Headquarters Company, 70th AACS Group."

October 5, 1944

Dear Folks,

I am quite settled again after spending a short while "down under." As I told you previously, I shall tell you some of the highlights of the trip.

To those of us here on Hawaii, the war seems much closer than it does to anyone in the States, if for no other reason, just the fact that we are out of the Mainland. To the boys right on the front, it means still more– it means exist the best one can– fight to live.

If there is any glory in the Services, it certainly is not on Saipan, Guam, or Palau. Out there the mud is a foot deep, the chow is "C" rations [individual, pre-cooked and prepared] when you are lucky, and the mosquitoes fly in regular formations. Dengue, Malaria, Jaundice, and filariasis are quite common.

When I was at Tarawa and Kwajalein, I thought it would be rather tough living there for any length of time. Most of the islands in the Gilberts and Marshalls are just coral atolls with little else than sand and more sand. The palm trees that were on these islands were all blown off by our naval guns.

These islands are a paradise, as far as living conditions are concerned, compared to those as one goes westward.

On one of the atolls, there are absolutely no showers or enough water to bathe. Soo– whenever it rains, everyone takes a shower outside. There are no women on any of these God-forsaken spots, but even if there were, no one would act differently.

There is one thing extremely noticeable where one goes, that is– no one seems to complain. Of course, they aren't the happiest bunch, but more than anyone in the States, they realize there is a job to be done.

The boys that were in the front lines are fighting– not to make this world safe for Democracy– but to get home again and lead a decent peaceful life. I would say that for 99% of these boys, the Army has educated them as only a war can do. I know whereof I speak, for I saw the situation in its true light. I was there!

If only the people back home would realize what these lads are doing, I am sure it would put many to shame.

Well, I guess I have sounded a little bitter, but actually I am damn glad I had the opportunity to see what it was like to go thru an air raid and crawl into a fox-hole for safety. I am not bitter– just disgusted about the whole situation on the home front.

Hoping that everyone is well, and Lewis is getting along as well as usual.

Love,

Herb

October 7, 1944

From: Army Air Forces

Army Airways Communication System

HQ, 70ᵗʰ AACS Group

Special Orders:

2ⁿᵈ Lt HERBERT I. BARNESS, O974522, AC, (0200), 70ᵗʰ ACS Gp, AAF, APO #953, is reld as Gp Weather Liaison Officer (PD) and aptd Asst Gr S-3 Officer (PD) effective this date.

November 23, 1944

From: Army Air Forces

Army Airways Communication System

HQ, 70ᵗʰ AACS Group

Special Orders:

Under the provisions of par 7d, AR 25-20, 3 July 1943, 2d Lt HERBERT I. BARNESS, O874522, AC, (0200), is aptd Group Claims Officer. He is specifically authorized to act as a Board of one Officer in any case within the provisions of Articles of War 105. Except for those cases requiring a Board of more than one Officer, he will also act as Investigating Officer, Board of Officers and Surveying Officer required by Army Regulations for the investigation of any accident involving death, personal injury or property loss or damage.

November 25, 1944

Dear Lou,

I hope you were able to enjoy this Thanksgiving with the folks at home instead of eating the well-known GI meal. We had a fine meal, but it just did not compare to any meal at home. As one fellow said, pot roast at home tasted just as good as turkey 5000 miles from home.

How are the women, nurses, and incidentally, the patients at the PGH? Do you still have that lousy old Dodge? When you get tired of the car, just send it out here and I'll sell it for about $1200. If I could pick up a car here, I think I would jump at the chance.

While writing this letter, am listening to all the all-star show from the States as they give-out for the men overseas. You probably read the criticism of Ann Sheridan when she was in the CBI theatre [China-Burma-India theater]. I saw the Bob Hope, Jack Benny, and Betty Hutton shows when they were out here, and must say I was disappointed in all of them. We don't get many stars out this way because they don't get as much publicity, and living conditions are very primitive on all outposts. I think the morale of the men would be much better if they filled those airplanes with cases of Scotch and bourbon, instead of those so-called stars from Hollywood.

I received a letter from Len the other day, and he seems to be having a rough time of it. The kid will probably get used to the service in the very near future– or he will never get used to it. Anyhow, he shall probably get a good education in the service.

My set-up here is about as perfect as anyone can ever find. If I could get a job in civilian life that is as interesting as this communications outfit, I believe I would think twice about it. However, if things are suitable, I still hope to go to Europe for reconstruction with Dad.

No other news,
Best of Luck,
Herb

P.S. Just heard that we bombed Tokio [Tokyo] (B-29's) from the Marianas– announced by Gen. H.H. Arnold in Washington. I saw this 21st Bomber Command outfit when last out west.

December 26, 1944

From: Army Air Forces

Army Airways Communication System

91st AAF BASE UNIT SECTION L

(70th AACS GP)

Special Orders:

2d Lieut HERBERT I. BARNESS, O874522, AC, (0200), 70th AACS Gp, AAF, APO #953, is reld Group Claims Officer (AD) and Group Morale and Special Services Officer (AD) eff this date.

CHAPTER 6

1945

LIFE IN THE SOUTH PACIFIC

In January, Herb noted that Admiral Nimitz had moved to Guam, and he suspected that his headquarters would also move. He noted that he had been in Guam before, in August of 1944, "when there were many Japs and lots of action." This was his only reference to combat. He made no other comments about this other than to say that, in 1945, it was no longer a war zone.

In April, Herb moved to the Marianas. The living conditions in Guam were challenging but he seemed to transition easily to life there.

Germany surrendered in May, but the war against Japan continued. In July, Herb was authorized to wear a Bronze Start on the Asiatic-Pacific ribbon for participation the Western Pacific Campaign (ground). He moved around continuously for about three weeks during the summer– to the Hawaiian Islands and to Canton Island– and then returned to Guam.

Finally the War ended in August! Herb planned to return to Bucknell and, upon completion of his degree, return to Warrington to work in the home building business with his dad.

Herb was promoted from 2nd Lieutenant to 1st in January, and from 1st Lieutenant to Captain in November.

January 1, 1945

Dear Folks,

Happy New Year! Today starts my ninth month on this island, and with each month bringing us closer to victory, it also brings us closer to home.

We had a rather lively and enjoyable New Year's eve celebration, but again there was that stateside atmosphere almost entirely lacking. The only similarity between here and the States was the usual alcoholic consumption.

Where is Marvin these days? Has he returned home yet? I guess upon his arrival in the States he will have completed his part in the war. As long as he returns safely, the Orleans' shall probably be none the worse for his experience. Perhaps, at long last, he shall get the opportunity to become an instructor.

Where is Gene– and in what outfit is he in? Let me hear from those fellows.

Love,
Herb

January 5, 1945

From: Army Air Forces

Army Airways Communication System

HQ, 70th AACS Group

Special Orders:

2d Lt TO 1ST LT:
HERBERT ISRAEL BARNESS O874522

January 7, 1945

Stationery of Lt. H.I. Barness

H.Q. 70th A.A.C.S. Group

A.P.O. No 246

c/o P.M., San Francisco, Calif.

Dear Folks,

Looking over my list of correspondence, it seems as though I owe just about everyone a letter. I think it would be much easier to just come back and stop all this unnecessary work.

Have you received one of the Xmas cards yet! I would just like to know how late they arrived.

Right now, as C.O. [Commanding Officer] of the outfit, I am living better than ever before in the Army. As I told you, I live in a regular 3 bedroom home with kitchen, bath, etc. Also have a 1941 Plymouth staff car to drive around. Know several Navy nurses and Red Cross gals so date just about every night. Sometimes even take off the day to spend at the beach. With all these comforts, I would still like to return to the States and school.

Love,
Herb

January 7, 1945

Dear Lou,

Received your letter that you wrote from home recently, which gave me a fairly vivid picture of the happenings at home.

I am fully aware of the fact that the folks are very worried about this kid, and for that reason I am going to give you a little advice– to wit: Stay in the States as long as you can. I was very anxious, as you can remember, to get overseas. Now as your time grows shorter, you too are probably straining at the bit to get some work done out in the field– do not let the propaganda fool you!

The war out here is much different from the war in the States, in fact it seems hard to believe that anyone back there knows what is going on. That isn't the tough part though; the tough part is the way they play the war up back in the States. One of my roommates, a navigator, has just returned from a month in California, and some of the stuff he has told us is quite disgusting.

You, like I, probably wanted/want the chance to get over so that if anyone asked you where you were in the war you wouldn't say, "Oh, I fought the battle of New Castle." Remember!! Well Doc, don't ever let that worry you because there are lots of guys who have done less.

I may sound a bit bitter, but I actually feel no bitterness. I am content, and I am sure if I ever had the choice (not that I had it in the first place) I would want overseas service. For me, it has been an education greater than I was getting in college. I have a position which is more than an Army job– if I don't produce, out I go to some desolate little coral atoll. But better than that, I have a job to do– and it is my first job other than working for Dad.

This letter is probably all mixed up and will not make much sense– I would have to talk to you to put my point across. That, too, will have to wait. Just remember though, lad, keep close to home to keep the folks happy.

Best of Luck,

Herb

January 7, 1945

Dear Folks,

The Air Force lost a great football game to the Navy today. It was, just as in baseball, an exhibition of the country's best athletes.

The weather has been extremely annoying recently with the temperature in the nineties. It is really very lovely, but the absence of snow in January, or even cold weather, is still surprising. You actually cannot imagine what this place is like until you have seen it.

How about sending a few of those pictures you said you were going to have taken? I shall be looking forward to receiving them in the very near future– or else!

Received a letter from Lewis in which he said things weren't quite the same at home since I have been gone. This was surprising in that I can't imagine things in Pennsylvania being the same since my departure.

Sometime in March it shall be a year that I have left that garden spot of the nation, and as things look now, it shall be several years before I return. I only hope that Lewis is permitted to remain in the States for the duration so that it may ease your mind.

Sitting behind my desk and pushing a pen around has added inches to my waistline, and other parts of my body. I must have gained at least 15 pounds since my arrival on the rock.

That's About All,

Love,

Herb

January 11, 1945

V mail

Dear Folks,

I fully realize that I have been very tardy with my correspondence– but naturally I have a good excuse; namely: work, sports, and fun. The work down here is as interesting as ever, and there is enough to keep me busy so that the time goes by rather quickly. One can hardly call it real work, for in my mind work was always physical labor. Here, however, pushing a pencil, talking to people, and traveling through the islands constitutes our labor.

Sports, on this island, are about the finest I have ever witnessed. As you have probably heard, we had the best baseball players of the major leagues playing for the Air Force and the Navy (usually spelled with a small "n"). During the football season (which ended last Sunday) again the Air Force and navy were outstanding. The country's greatest All-Americans and pro grid stars made their debut in the Hawaiian Islands. I might add that, in all sports, as well as everything else, the Air Force makes good that well known slogan: "NOTHING CAN STOP THE AAF!!" Now that basketball season is well under way, our own AACS is staying at the top of the league with all the other great teams.

I might delve into the sports situation a little further while I am on the subject, for as you may undoubtedly surmise, all forms of athletics interest me very much. The baseball season was over in October, although football began in September. Basketball practice commenced in November, while football continued into this New Year. And now that the basketball season has reached its peak, the Honolulu baseball league (in which service teams participate), announced its first game for January 28. The climate is absolutely the finest I have ever lived in, and this accounts for a year-round program of sports– enuf of that.

Entertainment, other than the above mentioned, is quite similar to that of those wonderful United States. Dances at the officers club, swimming parties, banquets, nightclubs, flying, picnics, women, surfboard riding, everything but snow and cold weather. Sometimes I wonder why they pay us on an extra 10% for overseas duty. Although many of the stories of beautiful Hawaii are strictly propaganda, there is still much truth to all the stories of the swaying palms and hula skirts, the beautiful moonlite sights, and the overpopulated city of Honolulu.

Although I have not exhausted my thoughts of Hawaii, I think it better that I sign off now. Will be expecting to hear from you soon,

Aloha,

Herb

January 15, 1945

Dear Folks,

This past weekend was one of many parties, women, and much joy. There was no special occasion other than the fact that we had no parties for about two weeks.

To answer your question of some letters previous: "I am still at the same place." However, you have undoubtedly heard of Admiral Nimitz's moving to Guam which shall probably mean that our headquarters will move also. Guam is not as good duty as Oahu, but it shall be pretty fair going. The first time I was on that island was last August when there were many Japs and lots of action.

I received your calendar and noted the additional telephone number under 6950. It may seem strange to you, but I actually forgot what our number was at home.

Nothing else new,
Love,
Herb

February 14, 1945

Dear Folks,

While I think of it, I might answer a few more questions for you: The rotation policy, or even a furlough, is not authorized in the Central Pacific until 24 months of continuous overseas duty. That means I have about 14 more months to "sweat it out" to become <u>eligible</u> for a furlough.

Gene shall probably be coming here, but let me know what you hear about him. If he will be on the islands, I will be able to see him.

Haven't heard from Lewis recently, but suppose he is rather busy. I haven't written to him for about two weeks, so guess I better do so soon.

No other news,

Love,

Herb

February 21, 1945

Dear Folks,

The longer I stay over here, the less there is to write home. News is very scarce, and you are undoubtedly tired of hearing of the weather of this place.

Have been playing quite a bit of softball lately, watching basketball games, and dating nightly. As a matter of fact, I find it rather difficult spending eight hours at work! This cannot go on forever so am making the best of it while I can.

Am getting a fairly solid sunburn after having peeled once this year already. Probably sounds fantastic to get a sunburn at this time of year, but that's the way it is.

No other news,

Love,

Herb

February 23, 1945

Dear Lou,

Long time no write– long time no see– long time!

I haven't been writing to you as often as I should, but as Mike Beshel once said: "He always has an alibi." I am not too sure, but I think this is the first time you have heard this one: "I am busy"!

With the rapid movement westward of our fighting infantry and Marines, those of us who are more fortunate to remain behind the lines must see that our buddies are taken care of. After having been to every damn U.S. island in the Central Pacific (except Iwo Jima), it may interest you to know that no one has ever dreamed of how true the statement "all Men are Brothers" may be. To clarify this I might say "All white men and negroes– but no yellow bastards." The boys out forward share everything, and except for the traditional service "brass," all men are equal.

I have been listening to the newscasts (which shall probably surprise the hell out of Dad– although I still dislike listening to any news while eating. After I got into the Army and I would ask Dad to change the station, Mom would always say, "Let him listen to whatever he wants, Joe– he won't he home long!") Anyhow– now to get back to my topic– the news reports coming from the States dresses up the battle for Iwo Jima, while the stuff we hear on the islands are offering a more vivid picture. There's a tough battle going on out yonder, and although people are quite confident of the outcome, we are still losing many lives. To you, a Doctor, lives are precious; and to those boys on the front, life is very dear!

As you can undoubtedly detect, I am in one of those "what we are fighting for" moods– but I'll be damned if I do know what we shall gain in the end. Enough of that!

You may remember a boy from Jenkintown by name of Gorham Getchell– played basketball against DHS, and then went to Temple. Saw him here last night when AACS trounced the Fleet Marines (whom Getchell plays for) by the score of 41-40! Marines were undefeated until they met the mighty mites of the Air Corps.

Have been doing a lot of daydreaming about home and some plans for the future. The best plan I can think of is to marry some rich bitch and relax for the next twenty years (raise a family, of course). There is always college to think about; also construction. Farming will be ideal for many servicemen, so the "Back to the Farm" move should cause a great real estate boom. Medicine entered my wee brain on several occasions, but ten years is too long a stretch at my old age. [Herb is 22 years old!] The war can't last forever, even though it looks as though it may- so we still have many days to do post-war planning.

Before you attempt to volunteer for overseas duty– if you get the chance– let me firmly tell you to stay in the States or I shall personally paddle your rosey-red-rectum. If for no other reason, you should stick close to home to keep the folks from worrying. I would just like to get home for about two hours so the folks could see I'm fat and healthy, and as good-looking as ever! Some of the neighbors from home have written and mentioned how forlorn Mom and Dad have been since I got overseas. The famous saying around here are, "You never had it so good," and "If your Mother could see you now she wouldn't believe you were in the Army." Both are very true in many cases, but the latter covers my case rather well. The moral of this story is: "Stay home Doc!"

It's getting later than hell and I'll be on the loose tomorrow night so better sign off.

Best of luck,

Herb

March 2, 1945

Dear Folks,

As soon as possible, I will have my picture taken and send it to you, but do not look for any for a long time. You have many pictures of me at home, so really no need for any more.

Next week shall terminate my second year of active service in the Army. In some ways, the time has passed rapidly, while in other respects, it seems as though I have been in the service all my life.

By now you should be enjoying some March winds and a slight tendency for better weather. We have no such seasonal change.

That's all.

Love,

Herb

March 11, 1945

Dear Lou,

Tomorrow I celebrate (?) my second year of active service in the Armed Forces. Time has passed rather quickly, but college, home, and civilian life seem like something hard to remember, and something a long way off.

Receive Les Trauch's address over here so shall attempt to look him up in the near future– in fact it must be in the near future or I won't see him on this island. Sometime soon we shall be fighting the war from the Marianas.

When we change locations here, I hope the folks will not fear that we are moving up to the front lines. You better impress them with the fact that [CENSORED] is no longer a war zone and although there are undoubtedly some Japs there, the situation has long been well in hand.

By the way lad, what say you send me some pictures of yourself, the folks, and some of the things at home. I have almost forgotten what everyone and everything looks like at home and I would really appreciate some pictures. If you can't get film, let me know and I shall send you some.

Oh yes, do you still smoke cigarettes– or has the shortage stopped you of that habit? If you need some cigarettes I will send you several cartons– but let me know soon.

Can't think of anything else to write now.

Best of Luck,
Herb

April 3, 1945

Dear Folks,

So Pop has joined the Coast Guard! Exactly what is his status, where is he pulling duty, and what sort of duty?

Seems strange to notice you mention that the weather is clearing up. In several weeks, I shall have a year over here, and in this time I have witnessed no noticeable change of seasons.

This may act as a request for a package.

Mail service has been very good lately since most of your letters arrive in five or six days– if mailed "air mail." Lewis wrote regular mail and it took about three weeks.

That's all,

Love,

Herb

April 5, 1945

From: Army Air Forces

Army Airways Communication System

91st AAF Base Unit Section L

(70th AACS Gp)

Special Orders:

Following named O and EM, orgn indicated, are reld fr further dy APO #953, and WP APO #246 for dy. T by first avail mil ap is auth. Baggage alws of sixty-five (65) lbs while travling by air is auth.

1st Lieut HERBERT I. BARNESS, 874522, AC, (0200) 91st AAF BU Sec M (Hq 70th Gp)

April 14, 1945

Dear Folks,

Fist of all, please note new AP0 #! I have now officially moved to the Marianas, and shall probably be here for the duration plus. It may interest you to know that we are on the other side of the international date line.

Living conditions here are nothing like those of Oahu. We are in tents with wooden floors (tents are 16' x 16'), outdoor showers where the water is carried and put in drums, old-time latrines, and many other forward-area conveniences.

The food is quite good, the sun is hot, and Sherman was right when he said: "War is hell." All in all, however, it's a new experience and conditions could be much worse- I have no complaints!

The whole island- everyone- is mourning the death of Roosevelt. I do hope it won't change the war or peace plans too much.

That's all,

Love,

Herb

April 15, 1945

Dear Folks,

Just about settled in our new tent- which is home for the duration. We have our office set-up and things are again running smoothly.

I disliked to leave Oahu only because I was having a fine night-life. Now I have no immediate chance for dissipation, and feminine companionship. It was definitely for the best that I moved, for many women fascinated me and I had spent another year there, I would probably be quite involved. Many hearts are waiting- I think!

The climate here is typically Pacific and am rather accustomed to it at this time. Went swimming yesterday at as fine a beach as I have ever seen. The movies could not film such a beautiful tropical surf.

Will write to Lewis soon,

Love,

Herb

April 16, 1945

Dear Folks,

Today is Monday here, and undoubtedly a very sad day in the States. According to news broadcasts, Roosevelt was to be buried today.

Things are shaping up very well out here, and I have had a chance to look around the island. It has far more beautiful scenery than Hawaii, even though the main town is practically flattened.

If it weren't so hot, I might contemplate some construction work during post war days, but after roaming around this long, I shall be content with anything in the States.

Wrote to Lewis today– at last.

That's all,

Love,

Herb

April 17, 1945

From: Lt. H I Barness

HQ. 70th AACS Group

APO #246, c/o P.M.

San Francisco, Calif.

Dear Lou,

Note change of address! Headquarters finally moved, and I am still pushing a pencil.

The Marianas, or at least this island, are/is quite beautiful. The climate and vegetation is strictly tropical with hot days, and rainy nights. We wear sunglasses at all times, and the usual tropical sun helmet adorns our cranium.

In our area the sun shines through the stalwart coconut groves which once belonged to some export company. The jungle borders the area where many Japs are said to have been killed. However, there aren't too many of the little fellows around any more, although several are killed daily.

The food is very good for a forward area base so no complaints on that score. Living quarters consist of a 16' x 16' tent with wooden floor. To urinate, one need only step out the door and aim in any direction–sometimes no-handed works. Latrines are those enjoyable three-seat jobs which forms calluses on one's rear extremities. It is difficult to enjoy a crap because two other fellows are usually sitting with assdown and head up!

Showers are also primitive– four barrels built on a platform approximately 10 feet high fulfills the water supply. Water is hauled in trucks and pumped by hand into the great reservoir. To wash, one need only turn on a spigot, fill a helmet, and proceed with the necessary motions. Shaving is a pleasure when good cool water is available.

Whether it sounds inviting or not, lad, I am having a great time. My only regret is that there is not chance for dissipation, and my nightlife is nil. I left Oahu after having fallen in love with several women, slept with several, and drank with all. Here I find that "Saturday Night is the loneliest night of the week."

By the way, I really think, at one time, I was quite serious with some broad (only she didn't put out) at APO #953. However, there is a lot of water between us now.

Well Doc, don't want to write too much so will sign off for now.

Best of Luck,

Herb

April 20, 1945

Dear Folks,

Am in the office now– have a few minutes– so thought I'd drop you a letter. There is, however, very little news that I can write at this time for once again, most of the news from here comes to you in the newspapers.

The boys here were extremely sorry to hear of the death of Ernie Pyle, who was becoming the regular "GI Joe" he was meant to be. Perhaps there are others, but none so famous yet. [from Wikipedia: Ernest Taylor "Ernie" Pyle (August 3, 1900 – April 18, 1945) was a Pulitzer Prize–winning American journalist, known for his columns for the Scripps-Howard newspaper chain, where he worked as a roving correspondent from 1935 through most of World War II.]

Went swimming here the other day and it was really swell– even better than Waikiki or Atlantic City! What a setting for a movie our beach would make– or what a setting for romance on this woman-scarce island. Everyone must be off the beach by 6 p.m. though, due to Japs lurking around the area.

Give my regards to all,

Love,

Herb

April 22, 1945

Dear Lou,

Once again your Pacific correspondent is giving forth with the news. Now that I have seen the clipping in the Intelligencer of my calling home, I begin to realize what a sad situation it must be back there when a telephone call is published.

Every once in a while, I hit the serious side of life, and begin to wonder what the hell I am going to do after the war. I would like to go into business with Dad, but I am not too sure he shall wish to continue after the war. Then I think my best bet is to find some rich bitch and marry her. That would solve many problems, if I can go through this battle without getting too involved with some dame. No chance of that here, but I left much behind at Oahu.

The situation here is quite stable with everything slowly taking shape. Our office is still set up in a tent, but we hope to get into our Quonsets soon.

That's all.

Best of luck,

Herb

P.S. Stay in the States!

P.P.S. Have you gotten married yet?

April 22, 1945

Dear Folks,

Received the clipping from the Intelligencer today describing my call to you. Seems as though everything is making news these days, so it's too bad I am unable to call from this base.

This afternoon I was attempting to grade our lawn in front of the tent. In the area, we possess an old Jap Caterpillar tractor and a wooden drag. It was lots of fun fooling around with the stuff again, and it brought back many memories. I do hope you still anticipate doing some construction work after the war because I'm sort of looking forward to getting in the game.

Looks as though the rainy season has hit us here so am going to plant another garden in this red earth. Melons, cantaloupes, etc. grow very well in this climate, which looks quite promising.

That's all,

Love,

Herb

April 24, 1945

Dear Folks,

Nothing new to write about from this side of the world but shall just let you know everything is going as usual.

Although you will not see me for some time, I might tell you that once again I have gotten my hair clipped to about 1/16". In addition, I have made an attempt to grow a mustache and have succeeded.

It is getting quite difficult to write home since I have been gone so long and really know little of what is taking place at home.

Love,

Herb

May 1, 1945

Dear Folks,

Received several of your first letters sent to this address. In case you are worrying about the change from Oahu, let your worries and cares pass, for with a bit of ingenuity, and a few quarts of liquor, we will have as nice a home as possible around here.

To illustrate my above statement, I may say that for one (1) quart of Shelley's Black Label (wholesale $2.15), we were furnished all materials and labor for an 8' x 16' porch (with roof). Floors are of plywood (3/4"), copper screening, insulated roof, and all accessories. Life is what one makes of it, and we are having a fine time. We lack for nothing.

Before I forget, can you please send me 200 sheets and 200 envelopes with my present name and address on the paper, plus my name and address in the top left-hand corner of the envelopes. Please do as soon as possible for I have no envelopes left, and they are very difficult to obtain– thanx.

Love,
Herb

P.S. Thanx for recent photos! Really appreciated the one with Dad in uniform and Lewis in civvies!

May 7, 1945

Dear Folks,

Working tonight trying to catch up on some of the back work. Business is picking up so hope we can end this damn war soon.

Each night, immediately after work, another fellow and I go swimming at the officers' beach. It's a lovely spot with typical tropical setting. Be a good place to open a hotel for tourist trade after the war.

Fixing up our place to look just like Oahu– only better! We have a bar now, painting the floors, and are building a grass roof. In several weeks we will be out of the tents and in good quarters!

That's All,

Love,

Herb

[On **May 8, 1945**, the Allies accepted Germany's surrender, about a week after Adolf Hitler committed suicide. Winston Churchill proclaimed it VE Day - Victory in Europe. This day marked the end of WW2 in Europe.]

May 9, 1945

Dear Folks,

Work every day, and swimming every afternoon (from 4:30 till 6:00) comprises the usual day in the Marianas. Most of the movies showing now are quite old, so I come back to the office at night to work or write letters.

Well, at long last, the war in Europe is over. Perhaps there were many celebrations throughout the world, but here there was no change of routine whatsoever. I now have hopes, though, of returning home by next May.

Finished painting our floor today, so will soon start on the mural on our bar. It's really getting to look like something after some diligent work.

That's All,

Love,

Herb

May 17, 1945

Dear Folks,

Have been quite busy the last few days assisting with the construction of pre-fabricated plywood barracks. I did everything from laying the floors, fitting windows, to putting on the roof. It was rather beneficial only for the fact that I am very much convinced that prefabs are of inferior quality to normally constructed dwellings, and I had a chance to fool around with construction work once again.

If possible, would like you to send me Tom Stringer's and Les Bowman's addresses, for I have reason to believe one of them is out this way. Haven't seen Uncle Jack's friend yet, but hope to do so in the next few days. Also want to visit one of my old college buddies who is in the same vicinity as the Colonel.

Life here has become very similar to that of Oahu, even so far as living quarters are concerned. However, there is always that distinct lack of feminine companionship, which was so plentiful in all previous fields.

Once again I am going to attempt to commence an extension course, but believe this may be more in the line of construction work rather than engineering. I cannot try to make any decisions at this time as to whether or not I shall return to college because there are too many obstacles now. I sincerely hope to return, and am sure this is my prime objective, yet upon consideration, many other opportunities seem inviting.

No other news,

Love,

Herb

May 19, 1945

Dear Folks,

Mail is very scarce coming into this island for some unknown reason, but hope things pick up soon.

Enclosed is a war bond that a fellow sent me from Oahu on V-E Day. I asked for a Lei Day bond from Hawaii, which is celebrated on 1 May, but due to the President's death, that holiday was not celebrated. So now I have just a regular bond that you can store away with the rest of the paper. This, as you know, is the first bond I have purchased for quite some time, since I have lost all forms of patriotism which involves buying bonds. I figure the people at home can buy the bonds and give blood to the Red Cross while the boys out here are expected to do everything.

Guess the majority of the family is again expecting to enjoy the coming summer at some resort. With Marv at home, and the war in Europe completed, I suppose the Orleans's feel that their share of the war is long past. However, I hope too many people do not have the same misunderstanding, for we are a long way from victory in the Pacific.

Suggest you talk to Lewis and try to keep him in the States for as long a time as possible and perhaps complete his internship and remain a civilian. This may sound as though I am contradicting my own theories, but I honestly believe it would be best for Lewis to keep out of the service at this time, if possible. The general consensus of opinion out here is that the doctors that get in now, just as any other men, will join the armies of occupation and spend several undue years in the Army.

That's all,

Love,

Herb

May 22, 1945

Dear Folks,

Cannot understand what the trouble with the mail situation may be, but there just doesn't seem to be any mail arriving from the States.

Just glanced through all the pictures I have taken and received since I left home last March. After counting them, I find I have the grand total of approximately 270 snapshots. The most of any one person I have received from home is of Mike Flitter. There are, of course, many relatives and friends whom I have no pictures of, but many do not bother me. I would like to receive some, though, of home, the setting of the house, garden, people, etc.

Received a letter from Dorothy, which I shall probably answer one of these days. How are the Saffiers anyhow? Guess this seems to be about the hay fever season for Auntie. Does Grace talk yet?

To answer some of your questions about Guam, I might say that most of the labor here is done by the service man. Labor is not cheap by any means, but rather money is very cheap and liquor is extremely high if purchased outside an officers' club. We pay about $1.60 per fifth of almost any liquor available. However, liquor is unavailable to enlisted men and they think nothing of paying from $40 to $60 a bottle. None of us would ever sell it—rather drink it ourselves, but whenever anything is desired, alcoholic beverages are a medium of exchange.

Cannot tell you too much about where we live, but there are absolutely no towns around. I doubt if you can visualize what the life here is composed of unless you were to actually see it. Night life is out of the question, and absolutely never thought about.

That's all,

Love,

Herb

May 27, 1945

Dear Folks,

Received several letters from you today, one of which contained a picture of a little girl. Hereafter, when you send pictures, and I do like to get pictures very much, I wish you would please tell me who the picture represented. It may seem odd to you, but you must realize that I have been gone for about fifteen months now, and children change in that time. Furthermore, most of the people and children were almost strangers to me since I have been actually away since March 1943.

I have an odd request to make at this time, and perhaps you can help. Am planting a lawn here, between the coconut palms, but grass seed is unavailable at this place. We can obtain all sorts of garden seed, as I have told you previously, but lawn seed is nil. Therefore, I will soon let you know if I can procure it in Hawaii, and if not, would like you to send some grass seed across these nine-thousand miles.

You asked me to take some pictures of homes while I am out here, but there would be no benefit derived by taking pictures of bombed and wrecked houses. There is nothing left here to take pictures of, except our own quarters, scenery, and other minor interesting objects. Photographs are prohibited entirely on this island for the present time, but we try to get a few of ourselves and living here to keep for reference after the war. The reason for complete censorship of photographs is that there are too many vital military objectives, which may blend into the picture. For instance, the everyday flights of B-29's may aid someone sometime.

That's about all,

Love,

Herb

May 29, 1945

Dear Folks,

Received a letter from Aunt Eva today in which she told me of some of the minor happenings of home. Surprised to hear that Rosalie is going to Penn State next fall. In the first place, State isn't exactly the best school in the country, and it accepts almost anyone who cannot be accepted at a college. However, times and people must be changing, so definitely concur that it is a very wise thing to send her to college.

One of my new-found friends on the island is the commissioner of one of the native villages. He is a native of the island, speaks rather good English, and is quite happy, as are all others, since the Japs have left. There is still a certain inherent fear all natives have for Jap snipers prowling throughout the island, but most Americans have the same fear. Out of a pre-war population of 25,000, he told me 200 were Protestants and the remaining 24,800 were Catholics. Each night they hold Mass, children attending first, then adults later. This must be done due to the fact that they do not have a church as yet, and must improvise as best they can. I was present this evening at 6:30 when their bells rang and the children flocked to sing the Rosary. It was very impressive to see children, whom the world thought of as uneducated and almost barbarous, to attend school daily, and to have Mass each night.

No other news,

Love,

Herb

June 29, 1945

Dear Folks,

Just came back from visiting Les Bowman who is preparing for his much awaited trip to the States. He has been overseas for the past 28 months so he well deserves some stateside duty. Les had just heard from Sonny Adams who is roaming the seas somewhere out here. Sonny has been promoted to the highest non-commissioned rank the Navy has, which proves that he has undoubtedly been doing an excellent job. I would certainly like to see him out here, of possible.

Something which may be of interest to you is the fact that the natives on this island have been doing much for the war effort. By government regulations, the maximum wage that can be paid for native labor is 16 cents per hour. This may seem almost absurd in these times, but if a man makes those wages, he will soon become one of the wealthier families. Anyhow, 16 cents an hour isn't very much, and yesterday while talking to the commissioner of the village, he told us that he was selling war bonds to the natives (yesterday) and out of approximately 150 people he visited, he sold $5000 worth of bonds!! This, to us, sounded amazing.

Haven't written Lewis in a long time so must get around to doing so in the very near future.

Love,
Herb

July 1, 1945

From: Army Air Forces

Army Airways Communication System

91ˢᵗ AAF Base Unit Section L

(70ᵗʰ AACS Gp)

Special Orders:

Following named Officer, 91ˢᵗ AAF Base Unit Sec M (Hq 70ᵗʰ AACS GP) APO 246, are aptd in the capacity indicated to act as a Unit Fund Council for this orgn, in add to their other duties:

   1ˢᵗ Lt (0200) HERBERT I. BARNESS, 0874522, AC, member

July 2, 1945

From: Army Air Forces

Army Airways Communication System

91ˢᵗ AAF Base Unit Section L

(70ᵗʰ AACS Gp)

Special Orders:

Under the provisions of General Order number 33, War Department 1945 and Circular 62, War Department 1944, as amended, the following named Officers and Enlisted men, organizations indicated, having served honorably and having been present for duty at sometime during the period 15 June 1944 to 1 May 1945 are authorized to wear a Bronze Star on the Asiatic-Pacific ribbon for participation in the Western Pacific Campaign (ground):

    1ˢᵗ LT BARNESS, HERBERT I 0874522

July 3, 1945

Dear Folks,

Want to take this opportunity to thank you very much for the very fine stationery which I received yesterday. It is indeed exactly what I wanted, so must thank you again.

Just completed a much-overdue letter to Lewis, which I am sending to Warrington, with hopes that you do not open it by mistake, and forward it later. Please deliver to him as soon as possible since don't know his new address.

Rainy season has settled in upon us and must wear heavy shoes all the time. When it rains in Guam, it really rains– not summer thundershowers, but a constant downpour for days.

Coming along fine with our home, and expect to have final touches added soon.

Also coming along fine with my mustache.

Love,
Herb

July 7, 1945

Dear Folks,

After work at night, we have been working for five, six, or seven hours per night on the house. It is looking very very good, and we are mighty proud of our efforts.

The rainy season is with us but actually isn't too bad yet. I understand it gets worse when the hurricanes and typhoons hit.

Saw an excellent show several nights ago– Dick Jurgens and his travelling Marine unit. It was far better than any USO show I have seen.

Visited Les Bowman the afternoon prior to his departure, so he should be able to offer fair knowledge of me upon his return.

Love,
Herb

July 9, 1945

From: Army Air Forces

Army Airways Communication System

91ˢᵗ AAF Base Unit Section L

(70ᵗʰ AACS Gp)

Special Orders:

1ˢᵗ Lt (0200) HERBERT I BARNESS, 0874522, AC, 91ˢᵗ AAF Base Unit Sec M (Hq 70ᵗʰ AACS Go), APO 246 is placed on TDY for approximately fifteen (15) days with 91ˢᵗ AAF Base Unit Sec A (Hq 7ᵗʰ AACS Wg) for briefing in Weather Relay Policies and Procedures. WP APR 953 by first avail mil ap reporting upon arr to the CO. Upon completion of TDY Officer will ret by first avail mil ap to his proper sta making a formal written report of his mission to the CO immediately upon arr. Baggage alws of sixty-five (65) lbs while traveling by air is auth (Cir 122 WD44). Auth: AAF Reg 35-59 dtd 15 June 45, ltr Hq AACS AAF dtd 25 Jun 45, 1st Ind 7th AACS Wg dtd 30 Jun 45 and radiogram 7th AACS Wg dtd 7 July 45. TDN. Officer is designated Official Officer Courier for the purpose of transporting classified documents necessary for the completion of this mission.

July 19, 1945

From: Army Air Forces

Army Airways Communication System

91st AAF Base Unit Section L

(70th AACS Gp)

Special Orders:

Following named Officers and EM are reld asgmt 91st AAF Base Unit Sec M (Hq 70th AACS Gp) and are asgd in gr to 720th AAF Base Unit (Hq 70th AACS Gp). No C in sta. EDCMR 200001 July 1945:

    1st Lt (0200) HERBERT I BARNESS, 0874522, AC

July 30, 1945

On Canton Island

Dear Folks,

It has been quite some time since I have written but as you can see, I am now a long way from Guam. For the past three weeks I have been moving around continuously, and as a result have neglected my correspondence. When I get back to Guam, I shall write and tell you about it.

Canton Island, in case you look for it on a map, is situated about 1600 miles southwest of Oahu. Will write more later.

Love,

Herb

August 1, 1945

Cablegram to Herbert I Barness 0874522 Amugdo Guam

NO MAIL WEEKS WORRIED PLEASE CABLE

JOSEPH BARNESS

August 4, 1945

Dear Folks,

I am indeed sorry and would attempt to apologize for not having written during these past three weeks, but existing circumstances prevented most writing except the letter which I sent you from Canton Island. I might tell you that I spent the early part of July in the Hawaiian Islands and it was indeed very very nice to be in civilization once again.

When I returned here I found many letters awaiting which certainly helped my morale quite a bit. Also received two packages from you with the olives, candy, peanuts, etc. Everything was appreciated by all– needless to say. I do believe my biggest enjoyment, however, was the photos that you included in your letters. It is always very pleasing to see the familiar faces and places of home, and the rest of the Barness family at home.

Noticed that Dad has a striking resemblance to Admiral Nimitz in the pictures, and several fellows actually thought it was the Admiral!! Mother is wearing anklets these days– probably due to the shortage of silk stockings, but I did not like the added gray hairs that are visible! Lewis is just as sloppy as ever as an officer– if you will note in the pictures his shirt–belt–and pants are not in line; his belt is not cut, therefore hangs about 8 inches too long; and his hat is not worn properly!!! Better give him hell for me when you see him again.

Well, can assure you that my letters will come more regularly now– but don't worry if once in a while they are sporadic. I can tell you that I am in the best of health and everything is going quite well.

Love,

Herb

August 6, 1945

Dear Folks,

Settling down once again to the routine ways on Guam, but no longer have my heart in the Pacific– or Army. It wasn't so bad being out here while everyone was around, but now that they are discharging quite a few men, I sort of envy those fortunate few. I guess my day will come sooner or later though.

This may act as a request for another package. Would you please include, if possible, one of those can-openers which cuts the entire top out. I think you probably know what kind I am referring to, and if we obtained one, it would be rather helpful.

Since you asked what we desire from home, I might briefly tell you that everything is appreciated, and it seems as though everything keeps well. Olives, pickles, candies, etc., are always useful, but one doesn't miss the luxuries out here. It is the little things of life which cannot be sent or procured that we miss the most.

Read in the Intelligencer (got about 10 of them at one time, Saturday) that Bill Satterthwaite was killed on Okinawa. If you want me to, I can visit his grave and probably speak to his commanding officer and friends. Of course, you will have to send me his former address and outfit.

Give my best wishes to Lewis.

Love,

Herb

P.S. Bought the enclosed Bond some time ago but always forgot to send it. Note date of purchase!

August 8, 1945

Dear Folks,

Nothing particularly new here except the news, as you have heard, of the atomic bomb. Don't know what this will mean because actually don't believe we dare use it too often. Perhaps we can get them to agree to peace terms more easily though.

How is Lou making out? I have written to him, but owe just about everyone else mail. This may act as a request for a package.

Love,

Herb

August 11, 1945

Dear Folks,

Have just heard the best news since I have entered this Army– the war is practically over! I certainly hope it is true for this may mean we return by Christmas.

You haven't told me much about your building plans but if you can't get the priorities yourself why don't you bear with Orleans until things break again. That is, of course, if he can get the priorities and needs someone to run an operation for him.

Please send immediately the negatives and prints you recently received from the censors. They all don't belong to me so would like to return them as soon as possible.

Love,
Herb

August 12, 1945

Dear Folks,

War news seems to be getting much better and we are probably getting much closer to home. Even though the war may end today, it does not mean that we shall be returning home immediately. However, if I am out here for more than six months after the occupation of Japan, without hesitation I want you to see our congressman and put a bit of pressure on him for my return.

During the war you have rarely heard me complain about anything in the Army, but once peace is declared, I want to get back to school and into business. Furthermore, I feel that I have served my time overseas, and since there are so many men who never left the States, I, like others over here, have the right to ask to go home. Let me know how you feel about this so in case I need some help from the home front, I will know your reactions.

Of course, all the above is pending on the termination of the war, and I hope it has ceased by the time you receive this letter.

Well, please send those negatives as soon as possible since I would like to see and return them. Also continue sending me photos of home.

This may act as a request for a package.

Love,

Herb

[From Wikipedia: Victory over Japan Day (also known as Victory in the Pacific Day, V-J Day, or V-P Day) is a name chosen for the day on which Japan surrendered, in effect ending World War II, and subsequent anniversaries of that event. The term has been applied to both of the days on which the initial announcement of Japan's surrender was made – to the afternoon of **August 15, 1945, in Japan**, and, because of time zone differences, to **August 14, 1945 (when it was announced in the United States and the rest of the Americas and Eastern Pacific Islands)** – as well as to September 2, 1945, when the signing of the surrender document occurred, officially ending World War II.]

August 15, 1945

Dear Folks,

While awaiting the news here last night, about 20 of us decided to begin celebrating a bit early in anticipation of the final surrender. The news flash was to come at 11 p.m. our time, which is 9 a.m. Tuesday your time, but even then nothing new had been added. However, by 11 p.m. the party was well on the way and the lack of any further developments did not dampen our spirits.

The pride in our home is ever increasing as we continually, but slowly, work on it. Now that the finish is near, we are ready to leave it for better lands we know.

Love,

Herb

August 16, 1945

Dear Folks,

Well, the long awaited word finally came from Japan and now we sit on Guam in a peacetime Army. It actually must be very similar to a peacetime Army for we have practically nothing to do any more. I have been reading several books and writing letters to pass the time away but am certainly going to get tired of it soon.

I realize it must take some time to get all the men back home but as I mentioned before, this is going to be the most unbearable time in service. I would really like to be on my way now and start school again next month.

No other news.

Love,

Herb

August 20, 1945

Dear Folks,

Quite wet out toady and since there is little work to do, the weather also dampens our spirits. With the war over, no more work to do, and no hope for returning in the near future, my morale is just about as low as it could possible be.

As a matter of fact, I think you better send me our congressman's address because I may want to write to him in the near future. As soon as I get 18 months over here (which will be in about 7 weeks) I might also ask you to put a little pressure on several of the big shots back there.

I called Betty Snyder today (Chick Snyder's sister– Ronny wrote and told me she was here) but couldn't get in touch with her. Will probably try again soon.

This may act as a request for a package– just received another from you which was very pleasantly enjoyed.

Love,

Herb

August 21, 1945

Dear Folks,

Found a Calculus book around the office yesterday so have begun to review the entire course. You cannot imagine what it is like to be sitting in the middle of nowhere with nothing to do.

Hope they start something soon on the rotation and demobilization policy very quickly because any sign of encouragement would be gratifying. There are men over here with from two to three and ½ years overseas who haven't even begun to think about going home.

My daily routine now consists of sleeping until 9 a.m.; go to the office for an hour or two; lunch; then swimming all afternoon. It's just like a big vacation and I wouldn't mind at all except that I want to get back and finish school. It is strictly a delay of time remaining here now.

That's all,

Love,

Herb

August 23, 1945

Dear Folks,

Yesterday several of my roommates returned from a trip and brought home a small monkey. As a result we have been enjoying ourselves watching him carry on and wondering if Darwin's theory is correct.

Am writing this from the office and am quite busy so will write more later.

Love,

Herb

August 25, 1945

Dear Folks,

At the time that the critical scores were counted (May 12) I had the great total of 38 points. This, as you can readily see, is too few to do much good. However, I get two points per month for overseas service, and if they ever have a recount of scores, I shall naturally be slightly higher. Also, there seems to be some talk of lower critical scores for discharge (present time 1st Lts. need 58 points).

Another point you might be interested in is that within the next two months I should be due for my Captaincy (necessary score for discharge 70 pts). However, due to the increased number of points necessary for discharge, I have requested to be suspended from any further promotions. The way I look at it– in two years from now it won't make any difference to me whether I was a private or a General in the Army.

Will try to do any damn thing to get out now that the war has ended!!!!!

Love,

Herb

September 6, 1945

Dear Folks,

This is the second letter I am writing today, so better not expect one in tomorrow's mail. It isn't that I don't want to write, or that I don't have time to write, but rather that there just isn't anything new to write about. Just imagine yourself on an island which is smaller than Bucks County and after going around and around the same spot for many days, it is quite apparent that after several days, the new news would be the same as the news the day before.

Many many months ago, prior to the time that we thought the war would be over by this September, my one desire was to return home for just a few days in this month just to fulfill an old promise. Had the war not ended, I was going to propose to my commanding officer that if he would give me five days home in September 1945, I would be willing to take any assignment he had and would not ask for rotation after my 24 months overseas duty had been completed. However, much to our great enjoyment and relief, the war has ended, and perhaps I will be able to get home for good in just a matter of months.

My only desire for giving up certain available privileges in this organization was my anticipation for being with you on your twenty-fifth wedding anniversary. We had been speaking of this celebration long before my entrance into the army, and I certainly wanted to be with you to enjoy the day which marked your twenty-fifth year of happiness. I can only say that I hope when you celebrate your fiftieth anniversary, any grandchildren that you may have accumulated will not be in another war because the job was not done well enough in this one. [Herb's parents celebrated their 52nd wedding anniversary by welcoming their first great-grandchild, Jennifer. Herb's dad died before their 53rd.] Of all the things I have missed most, I cannot think of any which would have meant so much to me if I could have been home for a short while now. I am certain that Lewis would be home if possible, and if he cannot come home, you shall be able to speak to him then.

I do not believe I have to express our sincere feeling and devotion for the many opportunities which you offered us, and the many sacrifices you so willingly made which would enable us to be better men and eventually attain the goal of your expectations. The human is so humble and dependent upon others that I hesitate to set forth any further means of appreciation for the enviable circumstances you have provided for us. It is only when one has been away and experienced some of the unfavorable conditions that were never thought of that one realizes that the little things of life mean so much more than the greater advantages. What may have been considered as little countenance by ourselves and others, at the time, now constitute the more practical aspects of human life.

The natives, Japanese, and Chinese always extend a deep-low bow when they wish to tender their appreciation, but the more civilized American merely says, "Thank you, may your lives be long and happy, and may we all be together again to enjoy the future days."

"Congratulations and best wishes."

Love,

Herb

September 27, 1945

Dear Folks,

Seems as though your plans for me, and the plans I anticipate, are very similar. First of all, I definitely expect to return to school when I get back, and upon completion of school go into business with you. I also agree with you that we will have to build on a larger scale and probably in many places.

When I get back to school I expect to have my own car, which may not agree with your desires, but I have two reasons for wanting a car. The main reason is that, with a car, I could get home on weekends and perhaps do some selling, thereby paying for the rest of my education. The second reason is that I have been thinking of getting my own convertible ever since I have been bouncing around in these jeeps out here.

That's about all,

Love,

Herb

October 5, 1945

Dear Folks,

The weather is so disgusting that it isn't even worth writing about. The mud is about a foot deep now and the rain just keeps pouring down.

Many fellows are going home for discharge but my plight still appears very bad. Just can't find any loopholes to get me out of here until they lower the requirements to two years of service.

Suggest, if you are interested, you contact someone back there about construction in these islands. I tried to find out from this end, but everything is being handled in Washington. I do know they expect to build about 8000 homes on this island, plus many more in the Philippines.

Love,

Herb

October 12, 1945

Dear Folks,

Last night a Lt. Colonel came thru here on his way back to the States for reassignment. I have known this man ever since I came overseas and we were quite friendly, for he was a good joe. While we were talking he asked me if I would like to stay in the Army and work with him at AACS Group headquarters in Reading, PA. I told him I appreciated the offer, but I did not want to stay in the Army. (If I signed saying I would stay in, I could get back but I would have to be in the Army till June 1947).

No other news,

Love,

Herb

October 20, 1945

Dear Folks,

Within the next month or so, three of my roommates are departing for home and I am sure they will probably call or drop in to see you. Their names are Jack Pennstrom (Capt.); Frank Sexton (lt.); Frank Perra (Capt.). All are from the East, with Pennstrom living closest in East Orange, N.J.

They, too, are departing with the flaming inspirations that" The Better Homes are Being Built by Barness in Bucks County!"

Received three (3) packages from you yesterday, some dated as far back as July. Also received the box of Salt Water Taffies– thanks for everything.

Love,

Herb

October 26, 1945

Dear Folks,

Enclosed are four snapshots taken inside our home "in the little grass shack." On the reverse side of the picture is the description of the place.

Also enclosed is a clipping about a book of buildings. Suggest you send for same immediately. This ad was in Time Magazine.

Also suggest you look into the selling of surplus equipment to veterans. I understand some excellent building equipment is being sold as cheap as dirt.

Love,

Herb

October 29, 1945

From: Army Air Forces

Army Airways Communication System

91ˢᵗ AAF Base Unit Section L

(70ᵗʰ AACS Gp)

Special Orders:

The following duty assignments are hereby confirmed. Any conflicting orders previously issued are rescinded:

   1ˢᵗ Lt (0200) HERBERT I. BARNESS

   08074522 AC

   Asst Operations & Requirements Off. S-3 (0200) (Pdy)

   Claims Officer (Add dy)

October 29, 1945

From: Army Air Forces

Army Airways Communication System

91st AAF Base Unit Section L

(70th AACS Gp)

Special Orders:

Following named Officers. AC, (W), 720th AAF Base Unit (Hq 70th AACS Gp) APO #246, are placed to TDY w/775th AAF Base Unit (Hq 70th AACS Gp) APO # 180 for the purpose of checking and inspecting AACS facilities thereat. WF APT #180 by first avail mil ap. Upon completion of TDY Officers will ret by first avail mil ap to 720th AAF BU (Hq 70th AACS Gp) APO #246 for dy. Baggage alws of sixty-five (65) lbs while traveling by air is auth.

1st Lt (2022) HERBERT I. BARNESS O874522

October 30, 1945

Dear Folks,

Received another weekly newscast from Mrs. Beardsley today, which was written on the 19th. I am now anxious to find out how your anniversary party was enjoyed?

Have been a little busier than usual since I am in charge of the Operations, plans and training section of this organization. This is the same section I have been working in for the past 18 months, but now I am in the boss's seat. I am not overly enthused about it 'cause I just want to get back.

Am well and happy– will write to Lewis now–

Love,
Herb

November 1, 1945

From: Headquarters

United States Army Strategic Air Forces

APO 234

Special Orders:

Under provisions of Hq AACS Memorandum 35-3 dated 16 April 1945 and 7th AACS Wg Memorandum 35-1 dated 18 July 1945 and Ltr Hq 70th AACS Subj: Promotions of Offs, dated 7 August 1945, announcement is made of the temp promotion of the fol named Offs of Army Airways Communications System to the grs indicated in AUS w/rank from date of this order:

1ST LT TO CAPT: HERBERT I BARNESS O874522 AC

November 14, 1945

Commercial Pacific Cable to

Captain Herbert Barness

Hq 70 AACF Gp APT 246

Amugdo Guam

CONGRATULATIONS KEEP UP THE GOOD WORK AND LETS SEE YOU HOME

LOVE
MOTHER AND DAD

November 21, 1945

Dear Folks,

Glad to hear that Lewis got home, plus the fact he may not have to leave those wonderful forty-eight states.

Lou said something about you contemplating going into the block business as a side-line to tie in with building. I think it is an excellent idea, but when you choose a site, it should be near a railroad siding to avoid any unnecessary handling of materials.

Also believe, if finances are available, a lumber-feed-building material yard would be ideal. By having such a company, plus a block industry, much more money could be made and saved.

I think these two businesses, plus actual construction, could be operated efficiently if all construction was given out in sub-contracts. This, to me, seems to be the only logical way of building. I am all in favor of a big concern, but not bigger than we can handle. If such a concern were built up, I think we could even work Izzy Saffier into a part of it, since he would definitely be conscientious. Better start speculating because when I get back I am going to be full of pep and vinegar to get things moving. I have even given serious thought to finishing school at Drexel so I could be closer to home and make a firmer foundation.

The government is selling surplus equipment to veterans, so perhaps we can pick up some new stuff, cheaply. I suggest you look into that a bit.

Although, as you know, I have never had a job elsewhere, I have enough confidence to feel that we could make a comfortable living by building better homes in Bucks County By Barness! My only regret is that I can't get home to start now.

I have been doing much daydreaming about our possibilities for expansion, so hope some of them work out. Perhaps my experience in the Army as a minor executive will help also.

Hope you are both well,

Love,

Herb

P.S. Please send me a package.

December 7, 1945

From: Headquarters

Western Pacific Base Command

APO 244

This is to certify that Herbert I. Barness has successfully completed the Western Pacific Army Olympics Umpire and Referee School.

December 8, 1945

From: Army Air Forces

Army Airways Communications System

720ᵗʰ AAF Base Unit (Hq 70ᵗʰ AACS Group)

Special Orders:

Following named Officers, AC, (W), 720th AAF Base Unit (Hq 70th AACS Gp) APO #246, are place on TDY W/777th AAF Base Unit (147th AACS Sq) APO #244 for the purpose of coordinating AACS Activities. WP APR #244 by first avail mil ap. Upon completion of TDY Officers wil ret by first avail mil ap to their proper sta APO #246 for dy. Per diem at the rate of $7.00 per day is auth under provisions of AR 35-4820 dtd 19 Apr 1945. Baggage alws of sixty-five (65) lbs while traveling my air is autho.

Capt. 0200 HERBERT I. BARNESS 0874522

December 14, 1945

From: Army Air Forces

Army Airways Communications System

720th AAF Base Unit (Hq 70th AACS Group)

Special Orders:

The following changes in duty assignments are announced:

Capt (0200) HERBERT I. BARNESS O874522 AC

RELD Asst Operations & Requirements Off. S-3 ((0200) (PDY) Claims Off (Add dy)

ASGD Executive Officer (0200) (PYD)

CHAPTER 7

1946

COMING HOME

By January, Herb was eagerly awaiting word on discharge and rotation. He was ready to go home. He wrote to his parents about Moke and Molly and contacted Bucknell University requesting re-entrance for the September term.

In February, he became Squadron Commander of the 147th AACS Squadron on Guam. He had about 1500 officers and men working for him. He had been the youngest executive officer that AACS ever had (27,000 men in the organization originally) and was now the youngest Commanding Officer of any AACS unit that had ever been in the Pacific.

In April he requested to be relieved of duty. He was not eligible for discharge, but he was able to do some extensive travelling and go to Japan to visit Lewis in May. He went to Yokohama, found his brother, and they sent a joint cable home to their parents! I can only imagine my grandparents' joy.

Herb returned home on June 24, 1946. One journey was over and another began as he returned to Bucknell in September.

January 16, 1946

Dear Folks,

No news of any consequence here, but am still awaiting some word on discharge and rotation. Hope you have written to the general, for I feel this may be of some help.

Just received another print of the "Grass Shack" for which I thank you. Please keep the negative when it is returned since I have some plans for getting an enlargement of it. What do you think of the place?

I thought I told you all about my monkey! He is just a little fellow who stands about ten inches high, and weighs about 5 pounds. He is lots of fun and a good companion so I expect to bring him home with me. His only fault is that he is not house-broken. I am getting a female monkey to keep him company, so will go into the "monkey business" when I return.

Love,
Herb

January 19, 1946

Dear Folks,

Last night a friend of mine and I entertained about 18 people for dinner and a sociable good evening. The most outstanding of the guests was the Bishop of Guam (an American) and two Fathers (Catholic priests). One of the Fathers was on Guam prior to the Japanese invasion, and he was taken as a prisoner to Japan.

In addition, there were several lawyers, women, and Dr. Brenizer (Lewis's friend from Mass. General) present. The Doc was completely amazed when he saw my quarters and staff car since there are few homes on Guam that can even compare to this place.

All-in-all, it was a most interesting evening. If the pictures taken turn out, I'll send some home.

Love,
Herb

January 24, 1946

Dear Folks,

The Colonel has returned from his trip, but he is leaving again for good on the 1st of February.

I requested a leave to go home, but it seems as though there are many fellows here who have longer overseas service than I. Therefore, I was told I could go back to Hawaii for duty, if so desired. However, conditions are quite comfortable here so I told them if I can't go home, I'll sweat it out here. As a result, on or about the 5th of February, I will become Squadron Commander of the 147th AACS Squadron on Guam. I will have about 1500 officers and men working for me so this should be good experience as long as I must remain in the service.

Love,
Herb

January 29, 1946

Dear Folks,

Spent the day at Saipan yesterday, getting together some things I will desire when I become squadron commander on the 2nd of February.

Although I want to get back to the States more than anything else, I felt quite flattered when I was told I was to become squadron commander. First of all, I am out-ranked by six other officers. This means I was just pushed ahead of some older, more experienced and higher ranking men. Secondly, I am the youngest C.O. [Commanding Officer] of any AACS unit that has ever been in the Pacific. These all sound good, but nothing is so good as stateside duty.

That's all.

Love,

Herb

February 1, 1946

Dear Folks,

This is the second letter I am writing today, which, as you know, is quite unusual. However, I received several letters from Lou which have left me in wonderment and unhappy.

First of all, he has indicated that both of you are feeling badly since I have been away so long, and now Lewis must go. I am certain you realize that neither of us wanted to be away for this length of time, but conditions are such as to prevent any interruption due to personal desires. Personally, I would gladly give a year's pay to be home again, but as long as I have to be out here, I am going to do my best.

Undoubtedly, you have been wondering what the idea is of my getting better jobs all the time. Well, some fellows have wives and children for whom they struggle to get ahead, get promotions, and try to be big shots, but when I knew I must remain overseas, I was determined to get the best possible so that you would be proud and you could tell everybody your son is a Captain, then became executive officer of a group, and now a Squadron Commander. Actually, I don't want this job I now have any more than I need two left shoes, for I want as few responsibilities as possible at this time.

I was the youngest executive officer that AACS ever had (27,000 men in the organization originally), and am now the youngest squadron commander. I might also add that I may be young in years but not in thoughts. I am certain this duty has aged me considerably mentally.

I don't want you to worry about me, although I suppose it is only, naturally, because I am in perfect health, live like a king, have many friends, and get along with everyone. Being in a command position, of course, demands everyone's respect, although I have been told many times that the respect has been given because I have treated men as men and not because of rank.

Enclosed is a copy of General Order number 3 stating my assumption of command.

Please don't worry.

Love,

Herb

P.S. Have you received the photos?

February 2, 1946

From: Army Air Forces

Army Airways Communications System

777th AAF Base Unit (147th Squadron)

Special Orders:

ASSUMPTION OF COMMAND:-- 1. Under the provisions of AR 600-20, the undersigned hereby assumes command of the 777th AAF Base Unit (147th AACS Sq), effective this date,. Vice Captain Robert S. McCollum.

Herbert I. Barness [signed]
Captain, Air Corps.
Commanding

February 5, 1946

Dear Folks,

Received the copy of the letter you sent to General Farman and believe it might do some good. It is difficult to understand what the war department is attempting today since in 90 days there will be <u>twice</u> as many officers as there are enlisted men in this theater. Our particular outfit will have 110 officers and 54 EM [enlisted men].

I hope Lewis can do something to remain in the States, but if I ever get back I think I know enough angles to play for the stateside end.

Love,

Herb

February 18, 1946

Dear Folks,

You have undoubtedly heard that the Air Forces intend to discharge 500,000 men and officers by 1 July 1946. This seems to be the best news so far on discharge so keep your fingers crossed, and I'll soon be home.

What's new at home in the way of building? Is there much chance for expansion of facilities and do some big building? Seems as though now is the time to make a killing with such a great demand for homes.

That's about all,

Love,

Herb

February 18, 1946

Letter to Bucknell University's Registrar:

On the ninth of January I submitted a request to your office for re-entrance to Bucknell for the September term. Since I am very anxious to establish definite plans for returning to school this fall, I would appreciate some answer to my previous letter.

Sincerely,
HERBERT I. BARNESS
Captain, Air Corps
Commanding

February 20, 1946

From: United States

Department of the interior

Fish and Wildlife Service

Chicago, Illinois

TO:

Collector of Customs,

San Francisco, California

Dear Sir:

In compliance with the application, dated January 8, signed by Herbert I. Barness, Capt. A.C., Hq. 70th AACS Group, APO #246, c/o Postmaster,

San Francisco, California, we are enclosing permit No. A505, authorizing him to import two monkeys, from Guam, expected to arrive either at the port of Seattle, Washington, or the port of San Francisco, California, on or about March 25, 1946

Permits,
Division of Game Management

February 27, 1946

Dear Folks,

Haven't written for several days for I have been unusually busy with all the enlisted personnel being discharged. I now have many Navy men working for me since we have merged communications facilities.

I hope building will improve and things will start rolling smoothly again because I am looking forward to building up a great Barness Construction Company. From the sounds of things, it is really tough to keep working, but I do hope you can manage. I wish I could get back to start some sort of work to help.

Lou told me of your plan to build an electrical appliance store. I, just as you, think it would be a fine idea. The greater expansion we have, the less cost for building items. Can't say much though until I do get back home– so here's wishing.

Love,
Herb

February 28, 1946

Dear Folks,

Both my monkey and I are getting quite tired of this overseas service and we would like to return to Beautiful Bucks County– where the Better Homes are Being Built By Barness.

The mail situation is absolutely terrible these days since very few aircraft fly in and out of Guam. I have been writing regularly but have received few letters from home or anyone else.

Have taken many pictures so will send some soon.

Love,
Herb

March 2, 1946

Dear Folks,

All the rumors around here seem to indicate that the category "5" officers should be released in the near future. If so, I should be one of the first to go and I'll certainly be home in May.

Still work every morning, swim and date in the afternoon, and drink and date at night.

Have met several Bucknellians here and make it a point to see them occasionally.

Love,
Herb

March 4, 1946

Dear Folks,

I have been working as little as possible here, but still try to keep the place going. Actually, my office hours are from 8 a.m. to 11:30 a.m.; then lunch– and I'm through.

As I have told you before, in the afternoons I date an Army nurse and we usually go swimming at the beach. About 5 or 6 nights a week I date a Navy nurse and we go out someplace for an enjoyable evening. Whenever I have some free time, I have a chat with my monkey.

Love,

Herb

March 5, 1946

Dear Folks,

Yesterday I received a letter from an old Bucknell friend with whom I have been corresponding for a long time. He has returned to school and is making some arrangements for my return in September. We plan to room together since we were both taking the same courses.

Also, yesterday, I received my necessary papers to return my monkey to the United States. Look for us sometime soon.

Due to some fouled-up conditions yesterday, I worked a very close schedule. I had a date with an Army nurse from 1 p.m. till 5 p.m., then with a Navy nurse from 5:30 till 10:30, when all women must be home. Today, one of the Bucknell boys I ran into here and I are dating a couple of USO girls.

Oh yes, found an old friend of Marvin's yesterday– an Irv Wolfe.

Love,

Herb

March 23, 1946

Dear Folks,

Irv Wolfe is departing tomorrow morning with one of my monkeys. He is bringing back the female, which he will give you. I suggest you build a small open-cage for her, and also have a place to tie her during the day. She might be a bit of trouble, but am sure you will enjoy the fun. [I remember my Mom-mom Barness telling us about the monkey, and how this animal kept biting her... but, since her son sent it from halfway around the world, she was determined to keep it until he returned home!]

Still no word on my possible return so am still waiting. When Irv gets home he will probably give the whole story of Guam and myself.

Love,
Herb

March 25, 1946

Dear Folks,

Took Irv Wolfe to the ship yesterday and put him aboard with my monkey "Molly." I hope they both get home safely.

By the way, Irv Wolfe is an optometrist, and although he was flying out here, he worked in the hospital part time. He fitted me for a pair of new glasses and believe I will go to him when I get home. Suggest, if you need anything done with your glasses, you patronize him.

Received a package for which I thank you very much. However, need absolutely nothing here so save it till I get back.

Love,
Herb

March 28, 1946

Dear Folks,

Nothing new here except we are waiting for a typhoon to hit the island. It's extremely windy and rainy but we have not felt the full fury of the storm.

Have been taking things easy as usual– still sweating out some word for return home and stateside.

No other news,

Love,

Herb

April 6, 1946

Dear Folks,

This is only the second letter I have written this week since I have been very busy.

Received a letter from Lewis saying that he is now on his way overseas. I was quite disappointed to hear of this, but guess it can't be helped.

As soon as you get his new address overseas– sent it to me! I am going to stay out here long enough to spend at least two or three weeks with Lewis to help him get settled and pass on any information I can. Also, if Leonard doesn't go home before that, I will see him in Shanghai.

My replacement will be here within a week so I could go back to Oahu or travel around here. I prefer waiting to see Lewis and spend some time with him. This way I will be home in June.

Love,

Herb

April 9, 1946

From: Army Air Forces

Army Airways Communications System

777ᵗʰ AAF Base Unit (147ᵗʰ AACS Squadron)

Special Orders:

Capt HERBERT I. BARNESS, 0874522, AC (W) (Primary SSN 0200) this org, dy W/Headquarters, APPO 246, is placed to TDY W/ AACS Det 44, APO 86 for period of approximately seven (7) days for purpose of inspecting AACS facilities. WP APO 86 by first avail mil ap and upon completion of TDY will return by first avail mil ap to proper sta APO 246 for dy. Per diem of seven dollars ($7.00) per day is auth. Govt shelter will be occupied when available. A reduction for four dollars ($4.00) per day for shelter will be made where such facilities are available.

April 9, 1946

Dear Folks,

Received word today that Leonard [cousin Leonard Caplan] will be at Saipan sometime this week so will certainly visit him. He must be on his way home since he is coming down from Shanghai.

Also received a cablegram from Irv Wolfe yesterday stating that my monkey is safely in the States with him. Therefore, you can expect to see her probably by the time you receive this letter. Hope you enjoy watching her– know all the kids will. Oh yes, you will have to keep her where no dogs or other animals can get her. Would advise putting her on a long line in the field, then build a little perch for her to run to. She should be kept in a cage at night. For full particulars, Irv can help you.

The name and address of the recipient of the check is:

Capt. Frank L. Perra
244 High Street
Westerly, Rhode Island

Frank is the fellow that called you when he got home.

See you soon,
Love,
Herb

April 13, 1946

Dear Folks,

Has the monkey arrived at home yet?

Hope to see Leonard as soon as he arrives at Saipan, so am awaiting some word.

My replacement has arrived and it is now up to me to decide when I desire to be relieved from this position. I expect to hold it for about another 10 days, or perhaps until Lewis arrives out here someplace.

I am not yet eligible for discharge so I would like to keep busy. However, I am going to start moving around again to see the Pacific next week so the following will be in effect:

I will write only once or twice a week from now until I get home! I am going to take myself some good trips and rest awhile.

Love,
Herb

April 18, 1946

Dear Folks,

Leonard's ship, the U.S.S. Samuel B. Moore, is anchored off Guam but am unable to see him because his ship is quarantined. He called me though, and I passed messages back to him. I tried to board the ship several times, but was unable to do so yet.

Received your letter about Ensign Dicker and shall look him up when he arrives.

My replacement has arrived at Guam since I requested to be relieved of duty. I am not yet eligible for discharge but I want to spend as much time as possible with Lewis. They thanked me very much for the job I have done, and told me I could write my own ticket from here.

I am going to do some extensive travelling, and may get stationed in Japan to help get Lewis settled.

It's a wonderful feeling to have received so much praise and be given an opportunity to do whatever I desire with my remaining time in the Army. I may even go back to Oahu for a while. The Colonel is going to try to get me a trip home through China and Europe, if he can do so. If not, I can fly straight back to New York from here when I am eligible for discharge. I will take the latter trip only if I can take my monkey by air. Otherwise I will go by ship.

In the meantime, I am going to eat, drink, sleep, and spend the day at the beach swimming. You can expect very few letters while I travel, and I won't feel badly if I don't hear from anyone too often because I will be travelling and won't get my mail except about once every two or three weeks.

Have much to write, but will see you in the relatively near future.

If you sent the $50 to Bucknell, I'm all set to start there on 16 September.

Love,

Herb

April 22, 1946

From: Army Air Forces

Army Airways Communications System

777ᵗʰ AAF Base Unit (147ᵗʰ AACS Squadron)

ASSUMPTION OF COMAND:-- 1. Under the provisions of AR 600-2, the undersigned hereby assumes command effective this date of the 777ᵗʰ AAF Base Unit (147ᵗʰ ACS Sq), vice Captain HERBERT I. BARNESS, O874522, AC, reld.

Nicholas T. Geeza

April 24, 1946

From: Army Air Forces

Army Airways Communications System

777ᵗʰ AAF Base Unit (147ᵗʰ AACS Squadron)

Special Orders:

CAPT (0200) HERBERT I. BARNESS O874522 AC (White) this Hq now at 777ᵗʰ AAF BU (147ᵗʰ ACS Sq) APO 246 will depart from 777ᵗʰ AAF BU (147ᵗʰ ACS Sq) APO 246 o/a 27 Apr 46 and WP 718ᵗʰ AAF BU (68ᵗʰ ACS Gp) APO 181 for TDY approximately thirty (30) days purpose of coordinating ACS activities and upon compl of mission will return to proper sta. Baggage alws of sixty-five (65) lbs plus an add wt of twenty-five (25) lbs for classified material is auth while traveling by air. Off is designated ofl courier and is auth to carry classified material relative to the mission.

April 26, 1946

From: Army Air Forces

Army Airways Communications System

777th AAF Base Unit (147th AACS Squadron)

Special Orders:

Capt HERBERT I. BARNESS, O874522, AC (W), (Primary SSN 0200) (Shipping SSN 0200) (MCO oo.999) (ASRS 51) (LAS 30 mos) (Category V) this orgn, is reld further asgmt and dy W/Headquarters APO 246, and trfd to 91st AAF BU (Hq 7th ACS Wg) APO 925, and is further place on thirty (30) days TDY with 718th AAF BU (Hq 68th ACS Gp) APO 181 for the purpose of coordinating 7th ACS Wg activity. Upon completion of TDY officer will return to proper sta, APO 925. Travel by first avail mil or Naval ap is auth to APO 181 and then to APO 925 upon collection of TDY. The provisions of 35-4820 as amended will apply. Officer designated official courier and is auth to carry classified material.

May 3, 1946

Now in Japan

Temporary address:

HW 68th ACS Group

APO #500, c/o PM

San Francisco, Calif.

Dear Folks,

Arrived here on the first of May- exactly two years after I got overseas!

Haven't seen Lou as yet but know his is somewhere in Yokohama which is about 15 miles from here. Will certainly see him next week.

This is rather good duty here so will spend about a month with Lou before coming home.

Don't write, as my return address is very temporary. I will write as soon as I can give you the correct one.

Japan is extremely interesting and much different than most other duty. I live in a regular hotel with all facilities, etc.

By the way, saw Len in Guam for two days. He has grown since I saw him last and he looks in fine shape.

Love,
Herb

May 4, 1946

From Japan

Dear Folks,

I have been offered a position with United Air Lines to start as soon as I get discharged. They will pay me $9000 for a year contract and I can get 30 days back in the States before starting. I would be doing the same kind of work I am now doing so I have a sufficient background. However, with all their inducements– I told them I couldn't accept at this time because I want to return to school. I might be making a mistake– but I couldn't spend another year out here.

Understand one can call the States from here so will look into the procedure. Can't get Lewis by phone so wrote to him at APO #502.

Love,
Herb

May 5, 1946

Dear Folks,

Having myself a semi-vacation here in Tokyo and enjoying all of it. The people and customs are entirely different from anyplace else I have ever been.

For the slightest favor one may do, these people continually bow and show all sorts of appreciation. Like in all occupied countries, a candy bar or a package of cigarettes will buy wine, women, or song.

As soon as I see Lou, I am going to hit the road again and do a bit of travelling. I will then return to Japan, spend more time with Lewis, and then come home. This will probably be in the latter part of June.

Love,
Herb

May 9, 1946

Dear Folks,

Tomorrow I am going to send you a Cablegram asking for Lewis' address, if you have it. However, when writing to me, use the return address as I have it on the envelope.

I am extremely confused about returning home and getting discharged since I still am not certain when I am eligible. I do think I will be home by the 1st of July, and at the latest in the middle of the month. If I can spend enough time with Lewis, I will probably hang around a while. At any rate, I want to get back and eat lots of fresh tomatoes (also lots of sour tomatoes– half red and good and juicy!); sugar corn; those big doughnuts; and lots of the delicacies we used to buy at that place on 11th Street (forget the name of the place). Although I have gained lots of weight over here, I am going to put on about 20 pounds more with Mom's cooking!

Love,

Herb

May 15, 1946

Western Union telegram to:

Joseph Barness

Warrington Penna

BARNESS BOYS HAVE JOINED FORCES IN JAPAN SAW LEW YESTERDAY LOVE HERBLOU

May 15, 1946

Dear Folks,

Guess it's about time I wrote you again since I haven't written for about a week.

Presume you have received my cable telling of my locating Lewis. I have never before checked, visited, inspected, and investigated so many places to find any one person. I finally found him by just sheer patience and perseverance.

I have no idea when I shall be permitted to return home as yet, but I am going to attempt to do some tall-talking to get back sometime in June. I keep thinking about all those fresh vegetables that I haven't even seen for over two years- in fact three years this season.

See you Soon,

Love,

Herb

May 16, 1946

From: Army Air Forces

Army Airways Communications System

91st AAF Base Unit (HQ 7th ACS Wing)

Special Orders:

The fol named Offs AC (White) this Hq on TDY Tokyo, Japan, are reld asgmt from mission and assigned for sta and dy with advance echelon, 91st AAF BU (Hq 7th ACS Wing), Tokyo, Japan, APO 925 off 17 May 46. No tvl involved.

   CAPT HERBERT I BARNESS O874522

May 21, 1946

Dear Folks,

Spoke to Lou yesterday by phone. He is quite well and waiting for me to come down and spend some time with him. At the end of this week I hope to go to Nagoya for about 10 days.

I received some mail today that was forwarded from Guam. The last letter I received from you was dated 23 April. I hope no more went to Guam because with my constant moving about, I probably won't receive them.

Glad you like Molly. She will be lots of fun always, but I know you can't house-break her. If everything goes as I plan, I will bring "Moke" home with me. Then we can really go into the monkey business!!!

That's about all,

Love,

Herb

May 25, 1946

From: Army Air Forces

Army Airways Communications System

91st AAF Base Unit (HQ 7th ACS Wing)

Special Orders:

CAPT (0200) HERBERT I BARNESS O874522 AC (MCO 00.999) (ASRS 61) (LAS 30) (Category V) this Hq is reld asgmt this Hq; is reasgd and WP 777th AAF BU (147th ACS Sq) APO 246 reporting upon arrival to CO thereof for sta and dy.

May 28, 1946

Dear Folks,

Am down here at Nagoya with Lou and will probably stay with him for at least another week. At the end of that time I am going back to Guam, pick up my monkey, and then take a boat for home. I hope to be back in Warrington by the first of July at the latest.

I will cable you when I depart from Tokyo and when I arrive at Guam. Also will cable when I find out my ship and time I will be in the States.

Thursday, Lewis is moving and I shall move along with him and return to Tokyo from his new location. I will write from time to time, but it isn't necessary to answer since I don't know where I will roam

I have read all the letters Lewis has been getting so am keeping up with the times.

Lewis and I have been discussing my possibilities of purchasing a new car. Since I haven't been home for quite some time, I am not too familiar with the financial standing of home. If a car can be purchased though, and you think I could use one, perhaps you can make arrangements for the purchase.

As far as I am concerned, I certainly would like to have my own automobile for many reasons, and I am also sure that it will prove beneficial. If you consider this favorably, I would like to have my first choice as a convertible– any make. I understand cars are difficult to purchase now, but perhaps your friend Nessinger, or someone else, can help. If you buddy, Ted Watson, has a Dodge, I would approve, although I would rather stick to the General Motors field.

I will leave the decision up to you, but be prepared for anything by July 1st.

Love,
Herb

May 29, 1946

Dear Folks,

Tomorrow, Lewis is moving about 120 miles from here to another smaller town. For a ground force organization he has a fairly good deal. Of course, it cannot compare to any part of the Air Corps, but being a Doctor, he has access to many things the other officers cannot procure, thereby enabling him to live comfortably.

Last evening we were having a long discussion of home and all the changes that have taken place. By the time I get back, I will have to spend several months just becoming acquainted with everyone.

I received the card you sent from Bucknell for my room choice. I sent it back to a friend of mine who is now at Bucknell, and with whom I want to room. He will take care of it for me. Also I shall probably drive up to Bucknell shortly after I get back home.

With further consideration on the possible purchase of a car for me, I have decided that if a new car is available, it would be best if you could put my name down for one. This, of course, depends upon the financial status of home. Any make automobile will be satisfactory, convertible type as first choice; two-door sedan second choice; color: light blue or gray. If a Chevrolet, Plymouth, Dodge, Pontiac, or Olds in not available, will consider a Studebaker, but will leave this up to you. Since I am not fully acquainted with the current situation at home, I will leave the entire choice up to you.

More and more I am considering going back to Bucknell for only one semester, then finishing at some school closer to home so I can work in the business, but this can wait until I get home for final decision.

Love,
Herb and Lou

June 6, 1946

From: United States Forces, Pacific

Personnel Air Shipment

Priority Clearance

Barness, Herbert I. O-874522 Capt. Permanent Change of Station. Cleared for air travel.

June 10, 1946

From: Army Air Forces

Air Communications Service

777ᵗʰ AA Base Unit (147ᵗʰ ACS Squadron)

Special Orders:

Capt HERBERT I. BARNESS, O874522, Ac (W) (Primary SSN 0200) (Shipping SSN 0200) (MCO 00.999) (ASRS 51) (LAS 30 mos) (Category V) this orgn, is reld asgmt and dy W/Headquarters APO 246, and trfd to 721ˢᵗ AAF BU (Hq 71ˢᵗ ACS Gp), APO 953. WP APO 953 by first avail mil ap reporting upon arr to the CO for dy. Baggage alws of sixty-five (65) lbs while traveling by air auth.

Stamp: Transportation via Naval Air Transport Service furnished from this station

June 13, 1946

From: Army Air Forces

Army Communications Service

721ˢᵗ AAF Base Unit (HQ 71ˢᵗ ACS Group)

Special Orders:

CAPT HERBERT I BARNESS O874522. C (White) (0200) (MCO 00.999) (ASRS 51-V) (Mo of sv 2 Sep 45-30) is reld from further asgmt and dy w/this HQ APO 953 is trfd stchd unasgd to Oahu Army Pers Center APO 969 and WP thererto form APO 953 for processing and further movement to continental US for separation from the service in accordance with current readjustment regulations. TBCAA. TDN. PCS. EDCMR 13 June 46. Off will comply w/A B Reg. 15—126 prior to departure from APO 953. Off will notify correspondents and published to discontinue mailing of ltrs and publications until notified of new address.

June 17, 1946

From: Headquarters

Army Personnel Center, Oahu

APO 969, c/o PM, San Francisco, Calif.

SUBJECT: Travel Orders for RH Personnel

1.   Individuals listed on reverse side will move from present overseas station on or about 17 June 46 to separation center in the United States to be named by endorsement to this order by the Commanding general of the

Port of Debarkation, for disposition in accordance with WR RRs. Each individual will carry his own orders.

2.   Individuals will be under control of the Commanding General, ATC, from time of arrival at the overseas ATC airport until released at The United States airport.

3.   Baggage to accompany individuals will be limited to 65 pounds.

4.   It being impracticable for the govt to furnish rations and qrs in kind during overland tvl FD will pay EM the monetary alws prescribed in Section II, AR 35-4810 for necessary period of such tvl. Per diem is auth within alws proscribed by law.

BARNESS, HERBERT I

O874522

CAPT AC

ARS SCORE 51 NO

MOS SSN 0200 4000

ADDRESS Warrington, PA

June 18, 1946

Western Union Telegram to Joseph Barness

DEPARTING FOR HICKAM SANFRANCISCO AND HOME FROM GUAM SPENT TEN DAYS WITH LOU LOVE HERB

[**STATESIDE!** On **June 24, 1946,** a Welcome Home sign greeted Herb in Warrington on this Monday morning.]

June 25, 1946

Certificate from: Armed Service Forces

Second Service Command

RECEPTION STATION No. 2

1262 SCU Personnel Center

Fort Dix, New Jersey

I hereby certify that on this date I examined CAPT. BARNESS, HERBERT I O-874522 and I found him free from any communicable, infectious or venereal diseases.

Signed, Lt. from Medical Corps.

June 26, 1946

Certificate from: First Army

SEPARATION CENTER

1262d SCU Personnel Center

Fort Dix, New Jersey

I, the undersigned, certify that the following are true and correct statements.

1. I have settled all my accounts with the following offices and have obtained the initials of the person authorizing to clear me in each section.

2. I have returned all government property and equipment issued to me and now in my possession prior to my departure from Separation Center, Fort Dix, New Jersey.

3. I have settled all my financial and property accounts to the best of my knowledge and belief.

June 28, 1946

From: ARMY SERVICES FORCES

SECOND SERVICE COMMAND

SEPARATION CENTER, 1262d SCU PERSONNCEL CENTER

FORT DIX, N.J.

Subject: Appointment under Section 37, National Defense Act, as amended

To: Herbert Israel BARNESS
    Warrington, PA
    Captain AC
    O-874522

The Secretary of War has directed me to inform you that by direction of the President, you are tendered appointment in the Officers' Reserve Corps, Army of the United States, effective this date, in the grade and section shown after A above. Your serial number is shown after B. above.

There is enclosed herewith a form for oath of office, which you are requested to execute and return promptly to the agency from which it was received by you. The execution and return of the required oath of office constitute an acceptance of your appointment. No other evidence of acceptance is required. Upon receipt in the War Department of the oath of office, properly executed, a commission evidencing your appointment will be sent to you.

August 31, 1946

Letter from Lewis:

Dear Herb,

Received your letter– on your new stationery–and am glad to hear that you finally got a car. Even though it's large, I'm sure you will enjoy it- but don't raise too much hell with it.

Glad to hear that materials are coming in a little better at home, and that building is proceeding on a little better scale. Incidentally, I've just completed my second dispensary since I've been in Japan– and will send you some photos as soon as I can get them painted. They are both conventional from the outside, but I'm rather fascinated with the floor plans, which are entirely outside regulations. The 89th has the better dispensary, but I corrected one thing in the 8th, so that I now have a private office, a lab, and a darkroom!

It's fun when you can build as large as you like and not have to worry about money. I was given a free hand by both battalions. My medics with the 89th are jealous of the 8th and vice versa.

Before I left Kobe, I played golf for the first time in my life, and in spite of a high score, enjoyed the game.

Also, I got in quite a bit of swimming.

Down here, there are some horses, and if the work eases up, I hope to learn how to ride a horse.

That's about all.

Take care– and lots of luck in your coming stay at Lewisburg.

Lew

September 19, 1946

On the stationery:

Herb Barness

Bucknell University

Lewisburg, PA

Dear Folks,

School started today with nothing particularly exciting happening. I have an 8 o'clock class every day except Saturday. On Saturday I have one class at 9 a.m. and am then finished for the weekend. On Monday, Wednesday, and Friday I go until 4:30, while on Tuesday and Thursday I finish at noon.

I was going to come home this weekend but I have several things to attend to, and I may date. I went out last night on a double-date with a friend of mine who goes with one of the profs' daughters. I dated a Jewish girl– for the first time!

Tell Rosalie to drop me a line and I may drop up to see her since she is only about an hour and a half from here.

2Please get out my typewriter and have it cleaned, for I shall pick it up soon.

Love,
Herb

September 24, 1946

Dear Folks,

If it is ok with you, I will definitely be home on Saturday the 5th of October instead of this weekend. By that time I believe I'll know what I may need for the next month or so during this semester.

I'll also know if I will continue onward this term, or I may drop out. It isn't that I can't do the work, or that I don't like it, but I'm afraid I'll have to spend at least 4 semesters to finish, which means February or June of 1948!! At any rate, I'll talk to you about it next week.

How is Lou? I haven't received any mail direct, as yet.

If you get the insurance policies ready for me when I get home, we can take care of it then. If not, perhaps you can send them up special delivery, and I'll mail them back the same way. This, of course, is dependent upon whether or not I am licensed.

Will also call this fellow Zink when I come home. As I recall, he wanted to start a millwork plant, so if you are interested, maybe you can contact him.

That's about all,

Love,

Herb

September 30, 1946

Dear Folks,

Happy Birthday Mom! [Actual birthday- October 3.] Perhaps one of these years we will all be together to celebrate some of these birthdays and anniversaries.

I wrote to Rosalie and told her I am going home this Friday so if she wants to go with me, she can let me know.

Received a letter from Lou today. He is quite well and getting along as usual.

If you can get 3 or 4 pounds of steak, or some other good beef, I would like to bring it back with me when I return next Sunday. I thought, perhaps Munz may be able to get some for you.

Also, it is getting cold up here so will want to bring back my Army jacket. Would you also give Haymann-Radcliff a call to see if my heater has come in for the car? If Watson has that convertible, don't bother about the heater—

Had a fine time Saturday at Cornell.

See you Friday.

Love,

Herb

October 9, 1946

Dear Folks,

This is the first chance I have had to write since I got back because I have been extremely busy. Every day this week, except Monday, we have had, and are continuing to have, tests. I have been diligently studying so haven't had much time for anything else.

How are you making out with the radio I ordered?

I was thinking about your wiring system in the shop and thought perhaps you should put the lighting system on one circuit and the other outlets for machinery on another circuit. This should offer some saving in wiring, and if your machinery shorts out, the lights will still be on.

Everything is fine and my cold has gotten all better.

Love,

Herb

October 19, 1946

Dear Folks,

This afternoon, the man who owns the riding horses out here asked me if I would mind taking out five girls and show them how to ride. It was quite a surprise, but I went out for two hours and made out very well– with the horse. It was the first time I had this horse and he was just like the frisky horse that Blythe has. I really had things under control though because I had to think of my pride. One time, my horse started running and didn't stop for about ¾ of a mile, running at full speed!! When I come home next week, I'll be all set to ride with you to Warrington.

Nothing else new,

Love,

Herb

October 21, 1946

Dear Folks,

Although there is nothing new here, I thought I would drop you a note.

Don't worry about my marks in school because I'm getting through ok. I was never a great student, and although I think I could really do well, I shall be content to get through as usual. The only difference now is that I am getting the most out of college, plus an education. As an example, one of the largest fraternities on the campus was working to get me in, even though they have never taken in a Jew. I was quite honored, but to prevent any hard feelings, I joined the Jewish group.

See you soon,

Love,

Herb

CHAPTER 8

1947-1948

THE FUTURE

Herb returned to college and once again his letters to his parents shared stories of his social and academic life. This was a time of transition, of making plans to join the family business, and of thinking about the future. In November 1947, he wrote about a woman he was dating frequently. This was the first mention of his future wife and my mother! In June 1948, Herb and Irma were married.

January 26, 1947

Dear Folks,

Glad to hear that Lewis may be on his way East next week. Am looking forward to seeing the kid again, and I guess you feel the same way.

As I told you, next Friday I'll be home for 6 days. The girl that will probably stay at our place for Friday and Saturday is Twig Taylor. She is the girl from Connecticut, but whose home is now in Kansas City.

Saturday night we are going to a basketball game in Allentown, to see Bucknell play Muhlenberg. Another girl, Gloria Anderson, will come into Philadelphia on Saturday afternoon, I'll pick her up, and then we will all go to the game. Bill Brooks is also going with us.

Gloria's date plays on the basketball team, and after the game he will probably come down and stay with us. The fellow, Francis Haas, Jr., is the son of the head of Pennsylvania's Department of Public Instruction (A politician, no doubt.) Look on your Real Estate License and you will see it is signed by Francis Haas.

Don't get the idea that there is anything serious between Twig and I, because I am doing this more for the accommodation of friends than anything else. I would also like to have another girl down for several days, but she can't make it.

Will get back to the books now,

Love,

Herb

P.S. Have wondered if you have the bar completed yet? If so, we will christen it!

February 20, 1947

Dear Folks,

Was very happy to hear that Lou is finally going to be coming home. Frankly, I can't see why he wants to fly across the continent, after coming to the west coast by boat.

As you as you hear from the Doc, whether it be day or night, give me a call and I'll head homeward as soon as possible. If you call during the day, just leave a message for me to call back as you did last time. If you call at night, and I'm not in, don't get the idea that I'm out dating all the time.

My dating is confined to the weekends, and only occasionally do I date during the week. However, there are other activities that I am in which take much time. I also have some rough courses this semester, and many of my nights are being spent behind a drawing board in the engineering building.

I have dated several more Jewish girls since I have been back, but I guess they just don't have any sincere Jewish girls here. All they want to talk about are their mink coats, homes in Florida, and apartments on Park Avenue. As a result, I have been dating Twig and have always had a good time.

I hope everything works out for the best in your new enterprise with George Klein, and I am sort of straining at the "bit" to get home to see if I can produce.

Will probably see you next week,

Love,

Herb

April 13, 1947

Dear Folks,

I have really been spending a great deal of time on my work since I have come back from Easter! The semester is over in six weeks and I want to clean up much work before then.

Here is the name of the lumber company in California:

Rocklin Lumber Milling Co.

Rocklin, California

Suggest you write to them as soon as possible.

Am still dating Twig but told her today, very definitely, that as far as I am concerned there cannot be anything serious for future intentions. I told her I was going to date around so it wouldn't get too serious. I know she was very hurt, so I am just going to gradually stop seeing her and by the end of the semester, everything should be finished. Until that time, I am going to cater to her so that she won't be hurt too badly.

I think this will please you.

I tried getting hotel reservations for you for May 10th, which is the weekend of May Day and Mother's Day. I couldn't get any in town so will probably stay in the next town, which is Milton.

Love,
Herb

September 20, 1947

Dear Folks,

Am completely settled here at school once again, but unlike last year at this time, I am not anxiously looking forward to a great year. Very little has actually changed, except of course, the usual graduation of old friends and faces which are no longer present on the campus.

If one were to view the situation from an outsider's stand, all facilities are available here to spend an excellent vacation. The social life is outstanding with the presence of six hundred coeds who seemingly brighten the days. The academic work is the simplest it has been for the past seven years, or at least since entering here as a freshman. Two days each week I must arise at an appropriate hour to enable me to arrive at class when the clock strikes eight. The other three mornings the alarm does not ring until several hours later so that I attend classes at ten a.m. Of course only the laborers work on Saturday, so I have no classes on that day. Sufficient recreational opportunities are at our disposal such as the College golf course, riding stables, tennis courts, swimming lake, and all sort of athletic contests to witness. Naturally, the elevation of this resort is such that it offers very healthful conditions.

When, then, look upon such ideal utopia with lack of interest?

Well, last year I was fresh out of the Army and thought the world was just full of money and good times and the well could never be pumped dry. However, after this last summer attempting to accumulate as much knowledge as possible about business, I was abruptly thrown into the facts that life on the outside was not as easy as I had wishfully anticipated it would be. It is not a finding of disappointment but rather of surprise, and it is this realization that brings further desires to continue quickly in work rather than vacationing for another four months. Do not misinterpret this in its entirety because I have no thoughts of stopping school at this time. Graduation is scheduled for the 31st of January 1948, and by the following June I shall probably wish I were back in school.

I would like to make some sort of financial arrangement with you in regard to my automobile since this automobile is for business. If you want, I will continue to pay my garage and maintenance bills and notify you so that it may be deducted. If you don't want to do that, let me know what is best.

I am in need of absolutely nothing at the present time with the exception of a few items I forgot at home. I will probably be back to pick them up within the next three weeks.

Bill Brooks did not return to Bucknell. Haven't heard from him yet so don't know where he went.

Have you sold any more homes? Has the bulldozer arrived? Did Marie send that sketch to Seyferts for the cutters? You better send them a door style. Has the Tenon machine arrived, or have you heard about it?

Love,

Herb

November 3, 1947

Dear Folks,

This is nothing short of miraculous! Two letters in less than one week! However, I have much to tell you.

First of all, I am going up to New York this weekend for the football game and wedding. Although I wasn't too anxious to go, I figure you are a little older and wiser, so I'll take your advice.

I am going to stay at Lou's home since he is going to the wedding also. We will get there Friday night and leave on Sunday evening. If you have any suggestions for a gift for Jesse, I would appreciate it, otherwise I guess I'll have to give him money– if you send me another checkbook. I have no more checks– which is probably a good thing, but I will need a book.

I have been spending too much money recently– and when it rains- it pours! The letter I received from you today contained a letter from the Veterans Administration telling me to remit $242.70 for my life insurance [$10,000 coverage], which was due on the first of November. I sent them a check so I hope it will be covered– plus the fact that we haven't received any checks from the government so I'll have to pay my board bill with your money. Frankly, I fell like hell about getting all this money from home, when I am way past the age where I should be making a living, but I hope someday I can repay you in some way.

Before you take the new truck out of the garage, please-please have a governor [Wikipedia: A governor, or speed limiter, is a device used to measure and regulate the speed of a machine, such as an engine.] put on it for 35 miles per hour. If not, this truck will be ruined also. I am anxious to get home to see what it's like.

Rosalie just called me. She is fine and sends her love. She is going home this weekend.

I have been dating around quite a bit this semester with both gentile and Jewish girls. It might please you to know– especially Mother– that I have been seeing quite a bit of one Jewish girl who is rather well liked up here, and whom I find very interesting. To give you a better description– she is quite attractive, a good student, a damn nice girl, and has a satisfactory financial statement– better than the 84 Warehouses. She has an older brother who graduated from Bucknell (he was here with me before the war), and she has a twin brother who is a fraternity brother of mine. She is my current flame so am having a fine time– will keep you posted on any new events. [This is the first mention of his future wife and my mother!]

I assume you sold the bungalow in the woods to the Doctor, and hope you sell a few more before the year is over.

Love,

Herb

November 6, 1947

Dear Folks,

If the weather is nice next weekend (the 15th), I would like to either come home, or have you drive up here for the football game and weekend. At this time you will be able to meet some of my friends and also the girl most likely to be your future daughter-in-law!

This will probably shock you very much since I have been running around quite a bit for the past several years, have had several current interests in women, but I don't believe I have ever gotten this interested– or at least interested enough in anyone to think I would like to spend the rest of my life with them. Being of sound mind and fair judgment, and after having looked around sufficiently, I am certain I have found the logical candidate to carry so great a name as Barness.

I suppose you might be a little interested to know something about the girl, so I'll give you a brief resume:

Her name is Irma Suzanne Shorin. Her religion is Jewish– a little more Jewish than I, but not much. I met her last year when I came back to Bucknell since her brothers are fraternity brothers of mine. She is not a beautiful girl, but she is quite attractive, has a wonderful sense of humor, graduates in June with a degree in philosophy, has a terrific personality, and is very very sweet.

We just like to do the same things and be together, which is just another way of saying we have a lot in common. Everything seems to be a meeting of the minds rather than any great affection and meeting of the lips.

Although it has had no bearing on my interest for Irma, she happens to come from a very wealthy family and has a great deal of polish. I can tell you much more when I see you since it is difficult to write a great deal.

As a matter of interest to Dad, she doesn't use any make-up, except lipstick.

In analyzing the girl, I tried to visualize your reactions towards her, and thus far I cannot see anything that you wouldn't approve of– except that she does smoke. I do believe you have enough faith in my judgment, and I respect yours very much, so I hope you will be pleased and not disappointed in the girl. Of course, you must realize, as I do, that your sons deserve only the best, and they are looking for only the best.

I am very interested in your reactions so please let me hear from you.

Love,

Herb

December 12, 1947

Dear Folks,

I have really been spending a great deal of time on my work this week so I can be a little bit ahead before Christmas. Irma and I have been studying together in the library, where absolute silence must be maintained, and things are working out well. As a matter of fact, I find it much easier to study, now that I feel settled down, than I did last year or at the beginning of this semester.

Our plans for Christmas are as follows: I will come home on the 20th. Irma will go to her home on the 20th. On the 24th she will come to our home and will stay until the 30th, at which time we will both go to her home for the remainder of the vacation. On January 4th we will come back to our home and leave on the 5th for school.

I want to thank both of you very very much for coming up here last weekend, and it was so much of a surprise that I can hardly realize you were here. It was indeed very pleasant and I sincerely hope we can continue to have such good times.

I bought Irma a Parker pen and pencil set– the best they make for $27. I know you weren't sure whether this would be good enough, but she needed a pen so I think this was sufficient.

Irma and I bought Eddie [Irma's twin brother- birthdays December 13] a cigarette case and lighter with his initials engraved, and will also give him the ties.

I wrote one check for $25 this week to pay my board bill and dues at the fraternity house since I paid some in cash from my regular check. I will also cash one more check tomorrow for $25 to take Irma and Eddie out to dinner for their birthdays.

Will see you next week,

Love,

Herb

Tell Lewis to come home for Christmas.

Please get me 75 Christmas cards with my name imprinted.

January 5, 1948

From: Veterans Administration

Regional Office

12 North Main Street

Wilkes-Barre, Pennsylvania

Because of the completion of your course in education or training on January 31, 1948, your subsistence award under the Servicemen's Readjustment Act of 1944, as amended, terminates as of that date.

We sincerely hope that you have derived full benefits form your course, and we take this opportunity of wishing you the successful undertaking of your future plans.

Your remaining period of entitlement to education or training benefits is 2 year, 9 months, 21 days. Should you at some future date wish to take another course to the extent of your remaining entitlement, you may do so by application to the Veterans Administration for a supplemental certificate of eligibility and entitlement. The law provides that a course must be completed by the end of nine years after the official end of the war.

January 12, 1948

Dear Folks,

Just spoke to the Shorin family, and they are definitely coming up here for graduation. I suggested that you all come up here together so I guess you will make some arrangements.

It's only nineteen days until graduation but it still seems a long way off. However, after all these years, I am really overanxious to graduate. I want to get out and get started as soon as possible so I can see what my capabilities actually are.

I was pleased to hear about the Doylestown property, although if you recall, I told you they would be glad to sell it to you. If we can grab enough men, we will be able to show Doylestown how real builders operate.

Don't worry about getting me anything for graduation– the new car and home will be more than sufficient.

We have been looking at many magazines on homes and have clipped out several good ideas.

I enjoyed the clipping in the paper very very much. As a matter of fact, would like to see the name of the town changed to Barness. We have always joked about it, but perhaps it can be done.

Will see you in three week.

Irma and Eddie send their love.

Love,

Herb

January 17, 1948

Dear Folks,

This, you should consider a true miracle. I have now written two letters this week!!

There are several things of importance that I wanted to tell you in yesterday's letter, but forgot to mention. First of all, please put a personal jewelry floater on my watch for $600. Irma's Mother told her she thought that's about what it cost, and I don't like to keep it here uninsured. Secondly, what do you think of the idea of sliding doors in the homes rather than swinging doors. I don't know if there will be any saving or more cost, but it is just an idea that I have seen in some magazines. Third, can you possibly get any linoleum in large quantities at a moderately wholesale cost? If I can get some linoleum (marbleized) at cost, I may be able to purchase about a dozen kegs of 8-penny common nails for cost (about $8.50) per keg. Please find out the price, and when I speak to you on the telephone, I will get all the details.

Eighteen days left until graduation!! I have come to the conclusion that although the Shorin children and us might have been brought up rather similarly, I am a little prejudiced in the fact that I think in many respects, we had a much broader and better background. Neither Eddie nor Irma have any ideas of responsibilities and their general habits are more as individuals than as society accepts. However, they are similar to us in the fact that their family ties are very close, and they have been taught to be very considerate.

I suggest that you get in touch with the Shorins, and if convenient for you, to have them come to our home sometime early on the 30th, so the four of you can get here on Friday afternoon. I will get everything arranged so that this visit to Bucknell will be at your pleasure, and there will be no check grabbing. That is, you will pay at the end of the weekend. Although Mother and Dad Shorin weren't certain that they could make it for the commencement, on Sunday, Dad Shorin assured me that they would be here. I am quite certain that they are as fond of me as you are of Irma. As a matter of fact, Mother Shorin told me that she never realized you could feel as close to someone else's child as she does to her own. Also, she said she wished that Joel [Irma's older brother] were more like me, but I think this was said only because they feel that Norma is pulling Joel away from them, since Norma is not close to her own parents.

Whatever you do, please make certain that you avoid all subjects pertaining to Joel and Norma, because you know much more about the situation than is good.

If suitable terms can be reached on the 1st of February, I shall be available for employment on Monday, February 2, 1948. The most recent offers I have heard other graduating engineers receive is as high as $293 per month, which is an excellent starting salary. However, I believe an equitable arrangement can be reached which will be convenient to all parties concerned, so you needn't worry about it.

I am going to write to Lewis and tell him not to attempt to come up here for graduation. This is the second letter to him within a week also. I am ahead of my work, so actually I have little to do.

Irma and Eddie send their love,

Herb

SEE YOU IN SEVENTEEN DAYS—After seven and one-half years this is almost better than returning from service, since I was always safe then, and I didn't have to go to work!!!!

January 18, 1948

Dear Folks,

Just a few things I forgot on the telephone conversation.

Better contact the Shorins soon and find out when you will be coming up for graduation.

Wrote to Lewis to find out about his plans for a trip to Bucknell for graduation.

Please send me all the literature you have, <u>by return mail,</u> on the machines to make nails. I would like to discuss the mechanical qualities of each machine with one of my professors who is a friend of mine. He holds a Doctors degree in Mechanical Engineering, and I would like to just observe his opinion of the equipment. He has spent several hours with me on my plans talking about various aspects of heating and ventilating, insulation, etc., in homes. I know if may sound foolish, but I am still interested. I have been reading about the building shortages for a survey, and I am convinced, items such as nails will be at a premium for at least two years in the country, and the export trade is overwhelming.

We went sledding today for a little more than an hour and had a great time. I am now weary, but feel very healthful. Both Eddie and Irma are in their rooms studying. I am through for the year except for studying for finals. I will probably do rather well this semester, but don't expect any honors at commencement. If I were as enthused about college before the war as I have been since I came back from service, I could have given you more honors, but that is all "water over the dam." Remember though, Lewis received nothing but a diploma at college graduation. I will be content with just that also!

Oh yes, we spoke to the Shorin family today, and they are all well. A friend of theirs (Ruth Green's inlaws- Ruth [Irma's cousin] is the young girl with two small boys now in California)- is sending us a gift of a set of Chinaware. This is a set of dishes. They're sending Joel the same.

Received a letter from the Kazarys [old friends and neighbors from Warrington, I think]. They are in Lancaster where Al is working for

Hamilton Watch Company. He is fairly pleased, but is ready for a change. They will probably be here for graduation if Anna May feels ok. Sure would like to use Al if we ever need someone else.

Irma and Eddie send their love,

Love,

Herb

June 15, 1948

From I. Shorin

582 Montgomery Street

Brooklyn, NY

Irma sent Herb's mother a seating chart for their upcoming wedding:

Table 1:

    Mr. and Mrs. Arthur Beardsley

    Mr. and Mrs. C.E. Mayer

    Mr. and Mrs. George Klein

    Mr. and Mrs. Elvy Crouthamel

    Mr. and Mrs. Lewis Troster

Table 2:

    Dr. and Mrs. Erwin Wolfe

    Mr. and Mrs. B. Flitter

    Mr. and Mrs. Eugene Sunshine

    Mr. and Mrs. Marvin Orleans

    Mr. and Mrs. Meyer Potamkin

Table 3:

> Mr. H. Schulman
>
> Mrs. Jacob Saffier
>
> Mr. and Mrs. I. Saffier
>
> Mr. and Mrs. A. Armel [Aunt Goldie]
>
> Mr. and Mrs. Leo Zuckerman
>
> Mr. and Mrs. Morris Caplan

Table 4:

> Mr. and Mrs. I. Lerner
>
> Mr. and Mrs. Julius J. Trumfer
>
> Dr. and Mrs. Jack Sugarman
>
> Mr. and Mrs. Joseph Beletz
>
> Mr. and Mrs. A.J. Sunshine

Table 5:

> Mr. and Mrs. Edmund E. Syme
>
> Mr. and Mrs. Edwin Satterthwaite
>
> Mr. and Mrs. Samuel Silverstein
>
> Mr. and Mrs. Louis Isard
>
> Mr. and Mrs. A.P. Orleans

Table 6:

> Mr. and Mrs. Martin Pollan
>
> Miss Miriam Beardsley
>
> Mr. Henry F. Suber Jr.
>
> Miss Marian Kreiger
>
> Mr. Howard Freeman
>
> Miss Rosalie Caplan
>
> Mr. Marvin Tomashower
>
> Mr. and Mrs. David Tabas

Table 7:

Mr. and Mrs. William Fortmann

Miss Betty Hoile

Mr. Robert List

Mr. and Mrs. George M. Romm

Mr. Louis F. Alessio

Miss Carol Griffin

Capt. And Mrs. Frank Perra

[Irma and Herb were married on **June 27, 1948**.]

ACKNOWLEDGMENTS

I am clearly not the "writer" of this book; I am merely the custodian of some precious family history. I thought about putting these letters together from the time I received them decades ago, and finally, finally I have done it.

First, this is a tribute to two loving, adventurous, courageous, strong, steadfast, patriotic immigrants who made their own American Dream. They brought up their two sons, farm boys, Lewis and Herbert, to become amazing men. To me, Mary and Joseph Barness, my grandparents, were the definitions of unconditional love. I was so lucky to have them through my teens and into young adulthood, as Pop-Pop lived to be 80, and Mom-mom to be 94. I have so many, many warm memories... from Mom-mom's candy drawer to Pop-pop's tears at every happy event. My parents, sister and I all lived nearby, and we shared many happy times. They taught me so much, and I have tried to model them as grandparents now that my own grandchildren have come along. I always knew I would be known as Mom-mom Barness, as a living tribute to these special people in my life.

Herbert Barness, the man I knew, was clearly a more mature version of the boy we met in his letters. Reading his thoughts as a boy and watching him change and grow through his own writing was quite a personal journey for me. The years after 1948 are the ones in which I learned about my dad, as I was born a year after this book ends. The rest of my dad's life, until his untimely death in 1998 at the age of 74, is another fascinating story. He accomplished many of his dreams and experienced many exciting chapters in his business, community, and even political life. But what always came first, always, was family. He would interrupt an extremely important phone call or meeting if one of his grandchildren called, and he would take that call without rushing– and with real joy. My father embodied so many of the qualities and values that his parents both lived and taught, and he shared them with us, his children and grandchildren.

The takeaway for me, as I gathered these letters, was something I always knew: Family First. That is the legacy of my grandparents and my father, and so I dedicate this book to their memory and also in honor of my children and grandchildren, as well as my sister and her children and grandchildren, who are privileged along with me to share in this legacy and carry it forward.

ABOUT THE AUTHOR

Born in 1949, Lynda Barness attended Warrington Elementary School in Bucks County, PA (and would have gone to a one-room schoolhouse if Warrington Elementary hadn't been built in time). She remembers the general store and post office in the building at the corner of Bristol and Easton roads, and has memories of playing in the cow barn and ice skating at the Garges farm.

Lynda graduated Phi Beta Kappa and Magna Cum Laude from Tufts University in 1971 and received a Master's degree in International Relations from the University of Pennsylvania the following year. She hadn't planned to go into the family business, but later that's what she did. She spent 13-plus years working with her dad for The Barness Organization, building homes and communities like her grandparents had done, only on a larger scale–just as her father had hoped. After her father's death, Lynda continued in the real estate business for another seven years. After she sold the business in 2005, she began an encore career as a wedding planner and founded I DO Wedding Consulting. She is the author of *I DO: A Wedding Planner Tells Tales*.